Table of Contents

The Invisible Chain

What is holding your business, or yourself from reaching your destined glory?

Introduction

Life presents how our parents think or believe it is the best for us and what they lack or wish to be. They could not become, or the righteousness of wealth creates a powerful mindset that will take us on our future path. Many questions arise, such as successfully achieving our dreams, living a happy life, and many other questions.

We see significant differences as soon as we interact with others and share ideas. They are based on our concept; we gather information and compare our current way of life with what has exposed us.

We may not be satisfied with our current lifestyle for several reasons. Sometimes our family has no evil intentions or did it on purpose. They have learned that their methods are just by exposition; for some of us, this will propel change and a massive desire for change for others. They only take what is given, and that's it.

This book gives information and hints about changing your reality and removing bad habits or actions that don't help you reach your goals. I can outline many of them, but we will focus on techniques to defeat harmful habits, procrastination, and fear.

It would be best to be held responsible for what is happening in your life. Most of us hate that part and do not want to get there. But, if you blame others, it's time to seek solutions and own your life, business, work, and yourself.

You can see yourself as a whole new person. Let's start by forcing ourselves to sincerely apologize for not taking good care of ourselves. And make many things happen by thinking you deserved it or they meant it to be. That will be your first exercise to break your invisible chain and change your self-perception.

Before continuing with the book's content, knowing, and understanding that our mindset is the key to overcoming change is important. You can have all the information for the world's most prestigious experts, but you must take action to achieve something.

My Story

When I was younger, I used to like sports of all kinds, and during the school year, my objective was to complete my schoolwork during breaks so that when it was time to go home, all I had to do was change my clothes and go back out. My mother, who used to police me, did not trust me at all, so she questioned me for the first two weeks, and when she realized that there was no missing homework, she let me go lightly. Also, if there was any doubt because of my last name, I was number one on the list, so... not doing homework was not an option; therefore, I trained myself to do homework whether they asked for it or not.

Being the first name on the list and participating in various sports helped me build a feeling of responsibility and get things done because results in both instances assess you. If you did poor homework for your assignment and are the first to deliver, you will be mocked by your classmates and receive a failing grade. You will not be selected for the team in sports if you do not consistently show up for practice on time and give your all on the field.

I am a living example that cultivating healthy habits can really transform your life. Habits are actions that we repeat regularly, frequently unknowingly. They might be positive or negative, and they significantly impact our lives. Forming good habits can assist us in becoming more productive, efficient, and successful, while breaking poor habits can help us avoid unpleasant consequences and live happier, healthier life.

Here's a summary of some of the most significant habits to develop, as well as how they can help you gain control of your life:

1. Wake up early: Waking up early can help you begin your day on a productive note, allowing you to do more while feeling less stressed. Every day I wake up at 5:00 am and read for 25 minutes. I occasionally write, view educational content, and do other things. That first hour of the day is all mine to do whatever I want regarding self-care and self-learning. Then, after 6:00 a.m., I get my three dogs, Douglas, Lizzy, and Coconut, ready for their daily walk and to clean up any nighttime messes that may have occurred. I leave my dogs at home after our

walk and head to the gym to do cardio and weight training. Afterward, I clean our apartment, head to the shower, and get ready to start my workday. I prepare my shake before beginning the workday and am finally ready to conquer my day! And, yes, I do have a wife and three children. I'm talking about a window between 5:00 and 7:00 a.m., and you can do it; no superpowers are required; just practice.

2. Regular exercise can help you stay physically and mentally healthy, boost energy, and improve your attitude. It is very true, and I genuinely want you to start exercising as much as you can every week; you may begin with as little as 5 minutes. And if you keep doing it daily, you will see results in no time. So many free exercises and routines are available on social media that you have no excuse. Incorporating this new pattern into your daily routine will help you feel more energized, eliminate distractions, enhance your metabolism, and sleep better. Be aware that the adjustment period may last three to four weeks, so be patient with yourself, and don't forget that

eating a balanced diet will help you keep a healthy weight, reduce the risk of disease, and feel like you have more energy throughout the day.

3. Establish goals: Whether you aim for personal, professional, or business success, setting goals will help you focus your efforts and stay motivated. The achievement of goals can stimulate the development of new behaviors, direct your attention, and assist you in maintaining momentum in your life. Objectives help in aligning concentration and fostering a feeling of self-mastery. In the end, you can't manage what you don't measure, and you can only improve something well-managed if you have measured it in the first place.

4. Prioritize your tasks: Prioritizing your tasks can help you manage your time more effectively and focus on the most important things. Prioritizing your chores at home and work can have many advantages, including A) Improved productivity: By prioritizing your tasks, you may concentrate on finishing the most critical ones first, allowing you to

do more in less time. B) Decreased stress: Prioritizing your duties reduces the likelihood of feeling overwhelmed by your to-do list. This can help you feel less stressed and more in control of your day. C) Better time management: Prioritizing your tasks will help you manage your time more effectively by allocating it to the most critical things first. D) Improved decision-making: As you prioritize your chores, you must decide which tasks are most important. This can help you improve your decision-making abilities at work and in your personal life. E) Improved focus: Prioritizing your tasks can help you stay focused on your goals and objectives, allowing you to accomplish them more efficiently. F) Increased sense of accomplishment: Doing your most critical duties first allows you to feel more accomplished and satisfied at the end of the day. I'm the number one fan of the Pomodoro technique of breaking tasks into 25-minute blocks; it really transformed my life.

5. Mindfulness can help you reduce stress, boost self-awareness, and improve interpersonal interactions. Mindfulness is a condition of being aware of your thoughts, feelings, and sensations in the present moment without judgment. Here are some mindfulness examples and methods to incorporate into your daily life: A) Spend a few minutes each day to concentrate on breathing. Sit comfortably, take a deep breath through your nose, and slowly exhale through your mouth. Concentrate on the movement of your breath in and out of your body. If your mind wanders, return your focus to your breathing. B) Mindful eating entails paying attention to your food's flavor, texture, and fragrance as you consume. Eat small portions and chew carefully, savoring each bite. Eliminate distractions like TV and phones and instead concentrate on the eating experience. C) Thoughtful movement: Exercises such as yoga, tai chi, or stretching can be done deliberately by focusing on your body sensations and the movement of your breath. D) Conscious listening: When someone is speaking to you, give them your full attention. Avoid multitasking and

planning out your following words. Please pay attention to their words and the tone of their voice. E) Walking mindfully means paying attention to the feelings in your feet and legs, the movement of your breath, and the sights and sounds around you. Strive to stay present and avoid getting caught up in ideas. F) Showering mindfully involves paying attention to the sensation of water on your skin, the smell of your soap or shampoo, and the sensations of relaxation and renewal.

6. Learn something new: You can keep your mind active and open new doors in your personal and professional life. Learning something new challenges your brain, which can help it stay sharp and boost cognitive performance. A) Personal development: Learning new things can assist you in developing new abilities, broadening your knowledge, and broadening your viewpoints. B) Improved self-assurance: You may feel a sense of success and self-assurance as you learn new things. C) Improved problem-solving abilities: Learning new things can help you build new problem-solving tactics

and approaches. D) Enhanced memory: Learning new material necessitates the usage of your memory, which can aid in improving your general memory skills. E) Discovering new things can stimulate your imagination and encourage creativity. F) Increased adaptability: As you learn new things, you may become more adaptable to change and more capable of dealing with new situations. G) Career advancement: Increasing your knowledge and abilities can help you stay competitive in the job market and develop your career.

7. Gratitude exercises can help you create a happy mindset and appreciate the good things in your life. The habit of focusing on and appreciating the positive aspects of one's life is known as gratitude. It is an essential component of mental and emotional well-being. Research has shown that it can bring various benefits, including A) Increased sentiments of social connectedness: Showing gratitude to others can help develop relationships and increase feelings of social connectedness. B) Concentrating on the positive aspects of

one's life can help alleviate stress and anxiety and boost general happiness. C) Improved resilience: Those who are grateful are more resilient and better able to deal with life's adversities. D) Better sleep: Expressing thankfulness before bed can help enhance the quality and duration of your sleep. E) Gratitude has been linked to improved physical health, including a more robust immune system, reduced blood pressure, and a lower chance of heart disease. F) Improved happiness and life satisfaction: It has been demonstrated that gratitude increases feelings of pleasure, life contentment, and general well-being. Gratitude is essential to living a healthy and fulfilled life.

8. Get sufficient sleep: Sleep is essential for physical and mental health, and it can help you feel more rested and rejuvenated throughout the day. Some advantages of obtaining adequate sleep include A) Increased cognitive function: Adequate sleep can improve cognitive function, such as memory, focus, and problem-solving abilities. B) Improved mood: Sufficient

sleep can aid in mood regulation and lower the chances of depression and anxiety. C) Physical health benefits: Obtaining adequate sleep has been linked to a lower risk of obesity, diabetes, heart disease, and other chronic health disorders. D) Sleep is vital for athletic performance since it can boost endurance, speed, and accuracy. E) Strengthened immune system: Sleep is vital for a strong immune system, which can help fight off infections and illnesses. F) Decreased stress: Sleep can help manage stress hormones, decreasing tension and overall well-being. G) Improved productivity: Obtaining adequate sleep might help you be more productive and creative and make better decisions. Remember that proper sleep is critical for optimal health and well-being. It can enhance cognitive function, mood, physical health, sports performance, immunological function, and productivity. Adults should strive for 7-9 hours of sleep per night to get these benefits, and I'm scratching the 7-hour mark, but I take 22-minute power naps throughout the day.

One crucial thing to remember during this new process is that you can begin with whatever item you like; the key is consistency and doing your best every day without cheating or skipping it. I have mentioned them because they have worked for me, and everyone around me can tell me about them. The idea is to create a timeline and establish goals for when you will complete the next one. We're not talking about years or months here but rather about weeks or days. Remember that you can learn or adopt a new habit in 30 days and make it a lifestyle in 90 days.

Here's an example of one of my habits. I decided a few days ago to see how many days I could read, so I bought an iPad, opened the books app, and began my reading quest. My initial reading span did not count if I read any pdf file, which was a setback. That worked only if the file was an epub document. I can't remember what my first count was, but this is the current count as of March 2nd, 2023, and I'm not sharing it to brag about it; I'm sharing it to show you that if you're consistent and do little by little every day, you can do a lot more. My time spent reading went from seven minutes to 25 minutes a day, and I have already read 90 books. Remember to keep pushing and never give up!

Most people, I believe, are discouraged by other people's accomplishments, and always attempt to find a way to put it off or tell themselves that this is not for them. I ruptured a muscle in my right calf a few years ago. My leg was stiff then, and I couldn't take a proper step.

I didn't understand what was happening initially because I was pulling our broken-down automobile to the side while everything happened. I thought about getting the car off the road and onto the shoulder. I eventually began to look at what had occurred to my leg after the automobile was relocated.

I didn't feel any pain, just discomfort because I couldn't bend my leg. When we returned home, my leg continued to hurt in the same way, so Diana, my wife, decided to take me to the doctor. When we arrived, they informed me of the rupture and advised me to seek physical therapy as soon as possible because it was not severe enough to necessitate surgery. They gave me painkillers and muscle relaxers.

Finally, we spoke with a physical therapist, who thoroughly explained what had occurred and the next steps. They estimated that recuperation would take 6–8 weeks, which seemed like a lifetime to an active person like myself. But that period has passed since I began to minimize the swelling and acquire mobility. Such agonizing sessions seemed to go on forever because the muscle was still sensitive and had bruises. After recovery, I could finally begin stretching exercises to aid my rehabilitation, something we had discussed for over a year. I gradually regained appropriate movement, which helped my healing process.

I wanted to tell that tale because it's important to realize that many things can happen to us, and it's up to us to determine whether they will impact our lives for the better or, the worse. Those physical exercises were terrible and left me with several bruises, but in the end, I wanted to heal to continue doing all I wanted. Keeping my mobility is vital because it is a critical reality as we age. I didn't want to have a physical disability because I was terrified of feeling pain and didn't want to do the work required for therapy.

I also get a therapeutic physical massage every two to three months. Forget the candles and Zen music; this deep-tissue massage entails exerting prolonged pressure on the deeper layers of your muscles and connective tissues with slow, deep strokes. My physical therapist is a woman who utilizes her fingers and elbows to break up scar tissue and alleviate muscle and tissue tension following my accident. And you are correct. I chose a woman because they hurt even more when made by men, but the important thing is that even though I know it will literally and physically hurt, I have to get it and do my part to heal myself.

That happened almost three years ago, and I still get some inflammation in my right calf now and then, but I'm still doing all my other physical activities, which was my original intention. Squats, for example, were a difficulty that has since passed. If we allow space for bad, tiny things to accumulate, they will grow into a more significant problem that will cost you a lot to fix. Remember that you are always in control. You can use little steps to achieve your goals one at a time. You can do it!

Explaining Mindset - Foundation

When we talk about mindset, it refers to the collection of attitudes, beliefs, and assumptions that shape an individual's thoughts and behaviors. It is the lens through which someone views the world, interprets experiences, and responds to challenges and opportunities.

Mindsets can be either **fixed** or **growth-oriented**. A fixed mindset is one in which individuals believe their abilities and traits are fixed and cannot be improved. In contrast, a growth mindset is one in which an individual thinks they can develop and grow their abilities and traits through effort, practice, and learning.

A person's mindset can significantly impact success, happiness, and well-being. Those with a growth mindset are more likely to be resilient in facing challenges, embrace new opportunities, and continue learning. Equally, those with a fixed mindset may be more likely to give up in the face of difficulties and struggle to adapt to changing circumstances.

Developing a growth mindset can be a powerful tool for personal growth and achievement, enabling individuals to overcome obstacles, take risks, and achieve their goals.

Can Procrastination and Laziness be referred to as an attitude or Mindset?

Yes, procrastination and laziness can be considered attitudes or mindsets.

Procrastination is the tendency to delay or avoid tasks that require effort or attention, often due to a belief that one can do them later or that they are unimportant.

On the other hand, **Laziness** is a lack of motivation or desire to engage in activities requiring effort or work.

Both procrastination and laziness can be attributed to a fixed mindset, in which an individual may believe their abilities or outcomes are predetermined and not subject to change. This can lead to a lack of motivation or willingness to take action, as the individual may believe their efforts will not make a difference in the outcome.

However, it's important to note that procrastination and laziness can also have other underlying causes, such as fear of failure, lack of direction or purpose, or even mental health issues like depression. In these cases, addressing the root cause can help individuals overcome these attitudes and adopt a more growth-oriented mindset.

How to Overcome Procrastination and Laziness

I have created a list of ten activities, or things to do that can help overcome procrastination and laziness:

1. **Create a to-do list:** Making a list of tasks and breaking them down into smaller, more manageable steps can help reduce overwhelm and increase motivation. Start with the most important or urgent tasks and work your way down the list.
2. **Set goals and deadlines:** Having a specific goal and deadline in mind can help provide direction and focus. Use SMART goals (Specific, Measurable, Achievable, Relevant,

Time-bound) to ensure your goals are realistic and achievable.

3. **Use a timer:** Set a timer for a specific amount of time (e.g., 25 minutes) and work on a task without interruption. This can help increase focus and productivity and reduce the temptation to procrastinate.

4. **Prioritize self-care:** Taking care of your physical and mental health can help reduce stress and increase energy levels. Make sure to get enough sleep, exercise regularly, eat a balanced diet, and take breaks when needed.

5. **Practice mindfulness:** Mindfulness techniques such as meditation, deep breathing, or simply focusing on the present can help reduce stress and increase focus.

6. **Get an accountability partner:** Having someone to check in with and hold you accountable can help increase motivation and reduce procrastination. This could be a friend, family member, coach, or therapist.

7. **Break tasks into smaller steps:** Breaking larger tasks into smaller, more manageable steps can help reduce overwhelm and increase motivation. Focus on one step at a time and celebrate each small success.

8. **Eliminate distractions:** Identify potential distractions (such as social media or email notifications) and eliminate or minimize them during work or study time. I know that today is tough, but at least set a block of time so that you can feel comfortable and gradually increase the time.

9. **Reward yourself:** Setting up a reward system (such as a treat or a fun activity) for completing tasks or achieving goals can help increase motivation and reduce the temptation to procrastinate. Please note, be wise with the kind of reward and try to stay within the time. For example, if you completed a task that took two hours, don't turn on your video game and play for 8 or 10 hours, say.

10. **Visualize success:** Taking a few moments to visualize yourself succeeding at a task or achieving a goal can help increase motivation and reduce self-doubt or anxiety.

Remember, overcoming procrastination and laziness takes time and effort. Start with small steps and celebrate each success along the way. With practice, these habits can become part of your daily routine and help you achieve your goals.

Motivational Manifesto

This manifesto aims to motivate you to use 10 activities to overcome procrastination and laziness. The 10 activities are creating a to-do list, setting goals and deadlines, using a timer, prioritizing self-care, getting an accountability partner, breaking tasks into smaller steps, eliminating distractions, rewarding ourselves, and visualizing success.

One of the biggest challenges we face when it comes to procrastination and laziness is feeling overwhelmed. We look at all the tasks we need to complete and figure out where to start. That's where creating a to-do list comes in. We can focus on one thing at a time without feeling overwhelmed by breaking down our tasks into smaller, more manageable steps.

However, more than simply creating a to-do list is required. We need to set goals and deadlines as well. When we have a clear goal in mind and a deadline to work towards, we're more motivated to take action. We can use the SMART goal framework to make sure our goals are specific, measurable, achievable, relevant, and time-bound. Using a timer can also be a helpful tool when it comes to staying focused and productive. When we set a specific amount of time to work on a task without interruption, we're able to increase our focus and productivity. It's amazing how much we can accomplish in a short amount of time when we're focused and motivated.

Of course, it's not all about work. We need to prioritize self-care as well. Getting enough sleep, exercising regularly, eating a balanced diet, and taking breaks when we need them are all important components of self-care. When we take care of ourselves, we have more energy and motivation to tackle our tasks.

Having an accountability partner can also be incredibly helpful. When we have someone to check in with us and hold us accountable, we're more motivated to follow through on our commitments. Letting ourselves off the hook is easy, but when we have someone else to report to, we're less likely to procrastinate.

Breaking tasks into smaller steps is another strategy that can help us stay motivated. Focusing on one step at a time makes us more likely to make progress and feel a sense of accomplishment. Celebrating each small success along the way can also be incredibly motivating.

Distractions can be a major obstacle when it comes to staying focused and productive. We can increase our focus and productivity by identifying and minimizing potential distractions, such as social media or email notifications during work or study time.

Finally, rewarding ourselves for completing tasks or achieving goals is important. Setting up a reward system makes us more motivated to keep going and avoid procrastination. Rewards don't have to be extravagant - they can be as simple as taking a break or indulging in a small treat.

Visualization can also be a helpful tool when it comes to staying motivated. By taking a few moments to imagine ourselves succeeding at a task or achieving a goal, we can increase our motivation and reduce feelings of self-doubt or anxiety. Visualization can help us stay focused on our goals and remind us why we're working so hard.

Finally, by implementing the ten activities suggested in conjunction with this manifesto, we may overcome procrastination and laziness and attain our objectives. It will not be simple, and there will be times when we will be tempted to revert to old patterns. But if we commit to these activities and remain motivated, we can do everything we set our minds to. So, let us take action and begin living the life we desire - one step at a time.

You will learn more about yourself as we progress. Working on the activities will help you understand yourself better, guiding you to the 2.0 version of yourself.

Chapter 1

"You cannot escape the responsibility
of tomorrow by evading it today."
Abraham Lincoln

Risk, Fear & Embarrassment.

We, the people in this modern society, have an amplified conception about many things involving "risks" to get started. Let's head back to ancient times. Any kind of risk could end your life or cripple you for the rest of your days.

You can easily relate when you watch and analyze an animated film called The Croods of 2013 https://www.imdb.com/title/tt0481499/ I will not tell you the movie. Still, a concept is giving, and most people forget about how hard it was in the past for our ancestors to gather their food and the risk involved. We give many things for granted.

Small things such as going out to seek breakfast can take you all day, depending on how you or they were with their hunting skills. Their survival was imminent. Also, they have faced change and fear because their world is changing, and they have no control over it; they have found an option for survival, and they have a choice to make it hurt or leave someone behind. Still, as always, you have to take your chances in life.

Besides all that, they were uncomfortable with the choice made; they were sad because of what and whom they left behind; others embraced change with joy (living the moment).

Everything wasn't easy or pleasant. But in the end, after really threatening situations, they survived and thrived not by their same old standards. Their journey took them to a new destination, and it was for the better.

This analogy about the movie can give you a solid foundation to get yourself prepared for change. Tear apart the chain that holds you back or start a process to leave your nest, your comfort zone, and seek and find new ground for opportunities that will take you to enjoy your life. This new life will make you happy, joyful, and glad about your decision.

Our modern risks are nothing compared to when we were younger at school or college. Our bet was a public shame (being embarrassed, not presenting homework, falling on the ground during P.E. class practice, and many more). For many folks, these situations have left a psychological scar. Even develop anxiety and other behavioral reactions that hold them from enjoying their lives or overcoming unnecessary problems.

Since we were little, we have had no clue what failure means or even exists. Nothing stopped us from exploring to crawling to reach anything that we could see; we had an endless desire to touch things we had accidents along the way. We learned what could give us a good experience and something we may not try again.

The risks of putting our little fingers inside the power outlet were tempting and even seemed like a game with our parents because they jumped on us to move us out of danger. We were innocent of many situations, but our learning process created a system to deal with risks. Those who caused pain as we grew—for example, smashing our fingers with the door and falling from our bike.

As life passes, we get the age to reach school (daycare, elementary, middle, and high school, or college) in our minds; fear is slight. We can say it is like a puppy for fearless people. It can grow to a Chihuahua size, but others can be as big as a Great Dane. As we grow, fear will change its shape and even look like a monster with superpowers if we don't learn how to control it and use it. Let's look at how many branches of fear you must assess if you are in control:

It looks to me like a two head monster with six arms and two legs, ready to disable us from all the good stuff in life, and if you don't learn to control this monster, it can drive you to make bad decisions. It's your call if you want to join the "avengers club" and defeat the beast and learn how to gain power. Remember, fear is part of us, and we can't get rid of it; the key is "control."

As the school year keeps going, we face new situations. We have entered the academic ground; those years were getting high fives from our teachers for writing our long-gone names. Now we need to meet the criteria for students of our age. Based on what we hear, building a good grade concept equals a promising future, opportunities, stability, grants, success, etc.

We can never measure the impact of those words and how they affect all youngsters at school. Some will do nothing, but others will leave a huge dent that could negatively impact when getting to adulthood.

Now we unveil what fear means and a possible consequence of failure. In academic terms means, not getting good grades equals did not meet the learning objective. But even if you earn your badges and approve the declared goals at the end of your senior year, you didn't achieve the minimum 4.0 required "G.P.A." You won't be accepted into your dream university.

No college equals no future! Maybe we don't hear that way, but for countless children, this means that you need to hit the streets and find a job because you have failed to meet the standard in the score to be accepted in college.

Many young adults felt left out and disable; the bus has left, and you are not in; What would you do? Run and try to chase it or sit on the curve and curse your faith? That is not the norm but is what society is saying. Maybe your parents don't share this concept, but you will deal with this all by yourself if they share it.

Perhaps this means now you have to develop a "logic plan" to conquer "Fear" in your life. That is a big chain you carry. It holds you to take risks, learn, live, enjoy your life, make money, pursue your dreams, have a business, or create startups, and be happy while enjoying your life.

We must learn to call things by their real name and not let negative thoughts root in our lives. Let's find what fear means: I have asked a trusted source for vocabulary at dictionary.com, and this is the result:
FEAR:

Noun
1. a distressing emotion aroused by impending danger, evil, pain, etc., whether the threat is real or imagined; the feeling or condition of being afraid.
2. A specific instance of or propensity for such a feeling: an abnormal fear of heights.

verb (used with object)
1. to regard with fear; be afraid of.
2. to have reverential awe of.

verb (used without object)
1. to have fear; be afraid: I'll go with you, so do not fear!
2. to feel apprehensive or uneasy (usually followed by for): In this time of economic instability, I fear for my children's future.

As human beings, we are curious by nature. But many people have lost this part of themselves while many love exploring. By attaining experience, we have learned to conquer our fears with our automatic self-preservation reactions. Any unpleasant or uncontrolled situation makes our heartbeat increase, our hands' sweat, have goosebumps, look pale, and have many more distressing reactions.

What is odd is that both people (those with fear and the fearless) have the same reaction meaning that in both cases, our body reacts in the same way. That is a mechanism in ancient times that has saved lives. For others, they became prey and bum! Game over.

In our modern society, we are not facing being eaten by a predator. Now many people are facing another kind of fear considered a condition commonly called "phobias." And what shocked me; was just doing a simple google search and typing "phobias list," I got a result of the "Top 100 Phobia list," meaning that there are too many. It Blew My mind away. Here you can see the results of my search on Google:

Top 100 Phobia List

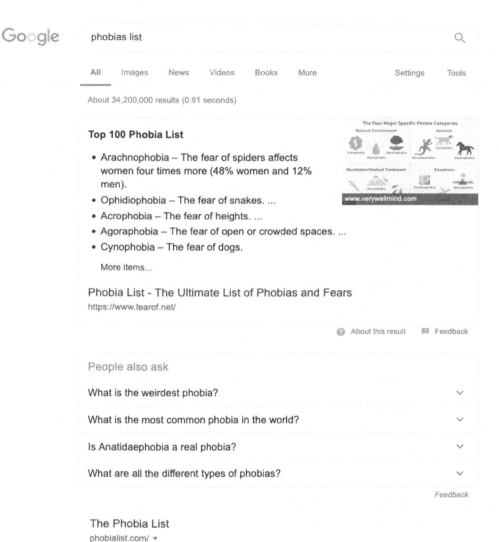

- Arachnophobia – The fear of spiders affects women four times more (48% women and 12% men).
- Ophidiophobia – The fear of snakes. ...
- Acrophobia – The fear of heights. ...
- Agoraphobia – The fear of open or crowded spaces. ...
- Cynophobia – The fear of dogs.

More items...

Phobia List - The Ultimate List of Phobias and Fears
https://www.fearof.net/

❓ About this result   ▦ Feedback

People also ask

What is the weirdest phobia?   ⌄

What is the most common phobia in the world?   ⌄

Is Anatidaephobia a real phobia?   ⌄

What are all the different types of phobias?   ⌄

Feedback

The Phobia List
phobialist.com/ ▾

When I started to see the results and read each one's meaning, I was shocked by how small things would become life-threatening.

The monster image shown above was nothing compared with what can be for many people. "Fear" is as enormous as the Kraken (The legendary Scandinavian, giant cephalopod-like sea monster). If they can't overcome this phobia, they need to seek treatment. Now, if you don't have any chronic fear (Phobia), we have a strong point about what it means: Why are you afraid to take risks at school, work, personally, and in business? You understand now that your life is not in danger, and I would like to invite you to try it now. You can start with small things, little by little until you have mastered them.

Let me share a little story of my own about fear:

I wanted to write a book a few years ago, and I was afraid of what people would think about it. The book's subject was about unveiling the truth about websites. Regarding what you see in your web browser, a strategy and research are oriented to a particular goal based on the audience intended to be delivered. I have been using the Internet since 1989, as far as I can remember. Since I have a technical background, I have learned a lot about it and started selling computers. I build them, deliver them to my clients, and provide on-site training, giving them additional service.

Eventually, the Internet made noise, and many computer owners wanted to access it. I sold a communication device called a modem, which uses a phone line calling the Internet Provider handshake equipment and granted Internet access. Those were the days of "dial-up Internet access." Then business kept evolving, and we entered the Web Development arena and built websites. Time passes, and the Internet becomes very popular. Other business owners didn't have much ethics, provided bad service, and scammed users.

Then I came up with the idea to write a book and got myself into the Indy race writers' arena. I did all my homework, getting ready my manuscript for the editor and grammar reviews. Then I got all the elements to publish my book. My professional fear kicks in, and then I question my book and get into the dilemma of what will happen if I'm wrong. What if someone with more expertise calls me a liar? "What if" was brought to my head, and it took me almost a year to publish my e-book on Amazon. I published the book on September 4, 2015.

The book is in Spanish, and the title is "La Verdad Sobre Los Sitios Web en Internet (Spanish Edition)." In English means "The truth about the Internet Websites," you can find the Kindle version on Amazon here: https://www.amazon.com/dp/B014WZWTF2.

What happened after I released the book?

Well, people loved it and wanted to work with my company. I have given it away instead of pushing online sales, which was not much. Still, we achieved profit by providing our products and services.

Like the book, people in the field may not even have many applicable technologies that have evolved. The market has shifted tremendously. But my point is that I did not let my fear of professional humiliation win. I have won that battle (even though it took me almost a year). My desire and intention are to give insights to break your invisible chain of fear and conquer your dreams, goals, and desires. The Kraken could have eaten lots of people, but in this case, you now have tools to learn how to manage your fears; you need not kill the Kraken. You just need to deal with it.

We can't get rid of fear because it's embedded in our DNA, but we need to learn how to gain control, which leads us to the next word.

Now let's try the word "fearless":

Fearless

Adjectives
    1. without fear; bold or brave; Intrepid.

The dictionary is correct about the idiom definition, but for us, honestly, it is not fit. A fearless person has mastered the ability to control fear, and to find logic to use in his favor. That is why we see people performing intrepid or bold maneuvers in several fields; fear is the fuel, making the difference in pursuing goals in our life.

Many of those fearless characters will keep doing or working to achieve their goal. For example, we can refer to Thomas Edison with the light bulb project. According to his biography, he performed 1,000 unsuccessful attempts at inventing the light bulb. If he quits because his invention isn't working, that is too complicated. Am I afraid to fail and look like a fool? Edison's quotes refer that he did not fail 1,000 times; it was an invention with 1,000 steps.

Many artists and performers face the same situation. If they have a hit on a painting, it will challenge them for the next one. How about musicians? They won't succeed in their musical career if they don't produce a great song. They are afraid of themselves because they have let insecurities take root in their lives.

Let's try to build a logical method to deal with manageable fears. Those who have reached medical conditions need to have more than a book to control them; they need to visit a psychotherapist. Maybe if you need, he can prescribe some antidepressants to reduce anxiety caused by your escalated fear.

Before starting to build the logic method to answer fear's call, try to understand what causes it:

1. Recognize fear and embrace it.

   As mentioned above, fear is part of us and can be harmful or useful; it is a mechanism that makes us react to cause a result. Having a better understanding is helpful, and we can generate leverage from it. As with every weakness, if you take action and overcome your fear, you can turn it into a skill, and you will lower your reaction to fear. Still, you must earn tons of confidence to pat your back and give you support when fear strikes.

2. Name the fear

The power of the word is unbelievable. When you let it out and mention your fear, you will sense a vibe, and suddenly you got the strength to deal with it. When you deal with your fear, this helps to shrink, but your fear will grow gradually if you ignore it. Think about that.

3. Educate yourself

In most cases, we are afraid of things we don't know, and we build an idea and believe it as a fact. When you learn about your fear, you will find information that will educate you based on facts. You will discover the truth about your fear; Knowing more about it will help you shrink it.

4. Know magnitude.

Let's be honest. How much have you let your fear grow? Chihuahua or Kraken size, you know you can deal with it. Whatever size it starts right now and make it smaller, don't feed the beast anymore is not helping you. You will face setbacks. We are not machines; we can't just remove fear and add a skill; those steps take time, but you need to start right now.

5. Have a positive attitude.

You need to work out your self-confidence muscle, the same as Edison did with the light bulb. He should have a colossal self-confidence muscle; being able to endure that journey to achieve a goal is admirable.

Many of us won't last that long when we face difficulties. From now on, problems as opportunities and not obstacles. Many issues are solvable except death; until today, we haven't discovered how to avoid them.

6. Seek help

That is a piece of cake. If you have assessed yourself as being afraid of something, you need to do this for your own good. Find whoever is available, even if it is online. If you need help depending on your fear, you can solve it with a coaching program or even a support group at your nearest church. Perhaps they could not be experts but speaking of your fear will be a great starting point.

As you can see now, applying a little logic to fears will make you strong, and you will gain self-confidence. Let's practice a few exercises:

Are you afraid of:

- Speaking in public – Find a course online, a mentor, or a coach, and practice with your friends.

- Being jobless – Give yourself 100% every day, do your best in your situation, and own your position. Holding your position will open opportunities for promotion. If you are already on edge or hate your job, start right now by preparing to find a new opening in another company or create your own. You want to be better; You can find programs to boost productivity at work; There are many ways to reach them.

- Having lots of money – This one is easy; If you have money, you can help anyone. If you are worried about being greedy, you are already concerned, and it will be easier to maintain control. Keep your mind focused on your goals. Don't let your ego spike and make you greedy; read about minimalism and be grounded.

- Professional humiliation – We all are smart individuals. Each one of us has our talents and gifts. The beauty is that all of us have different opinions. Some would like your idea; others don't, and based on what you are presenting, they will love or hate the idea. In most cases, it is not about the good you are giving is the consequence for others that may cause rejection. If you follow the steps, do what you are being asked to, and do diligent and thrilling work, I'm sure you will not have to fear this situation.

- Losing your home - Well, this is about payments, and if you are afraid of losing your sweet home, there is a solution. First, you can talk to the bank to see if you can reduce payments if you are short in cash or refinance. Then you need to make your check and balances assessment to find out where your money is leaking and solve the problem.

As you can see, I can build a massive list of logical solutions for most of our problems. You need to act and stop your fear from growing, cut all the roots and branches, and not feed fear anymore; enough is enough.

Pursuing Goals

That is one of the most complex tasks we have ever been told; they gave many of us a script of what it should be an achiever, but the whole concept is so broad that we can't see the end of the line; We must keep going.

Life was simple and beautiful; we enjoyed our days more, tasks were easy to achieve, and goals seemed reachable.

Having a simple life was joyful; our small responsibilities were the obstacle we had, and fulfilling our duties would release all the available rewards. Maybe we didn't complain about it, rolling our eyes without being caught by our parents because our focus was the prize.

All rewards were different. A prize could enjoy a piece of chocolate, playing Xbox or PlayStation, going to the park, riding on a bike, playing at the pool, and name it. As soon as we mature, our goals shift to rewards; our innocence must face reality.

Goals in life need to be a message well delivered. With intention and purpose, many people stuck with his invisible chain got their message after a discussion. It's heartbreaking receiving this word:

Here is an example:

- Get a degree

- Get a good and stable job
- Don't get in trouble
- Find a good spouse
- Save, save!

We are receiving a message without context. That develops in a context-less goal because we want to please our parents or deliver that message. Avoid making room for the fear monster.

Most life goals are achievable if you have a system and push yourself to complete all steps involved. Here you will find golden tips to achieve goals in life.

1. Set goals that motivate you.

   The whole idea of goal setting is pursuing something that encourages you to work on it. Anything you desire to accomplish needs to have a process, breaking it down into small achievable milestones.

   Then, each milestone contains several small tasks that will give you a part of your goal finished when completed. You can be overwhelmed and quit quickly if you don't plan in small steps.

2. Write and read your goals out loud.

Do your homework and write what you want. Inspect and make sure you got it right; The next step is invoking "the word's power." When you read aloud, the energy sends a prep talk to your body, and it pumps you, excited and motivated.

Suppose you don't feel it or don't have the inspiration. Ensure you set the right environment, favorite music, or movie that brings you joy and allows you to dream and chase achievable life goals. Make sure you do it, don't put it off.

3. Build a plan.

Once you have done your homework, it's time to get busy. Building a plan is the best way to organize the work coming ahead. You need to commit time and resources to meet each milestone of your goal.

A dream without action is just a desire. Suppose you have issues managing your time and fulfilling goals. You can visit this website getyourselfontime.com and get help; Don't use defeat words. It doesn't matter how old or young you are, and you deserve to reach your goals in life; It does not mean you work just to pay your bills.

4. Practice self-control.

With your plan in place, you have deadlines to meet, meaning you need to stick to your schedule to fulfill each task outlined when building your dream.

Assume you do not meet those dates because you got distracted, bored, etc. That means you need to straight-up your self-control habits and push yourself to do it. You are building a new habit and will have setbacks; We are not machines.

It doesn't matter how tired you are after work; instead, do it when the day starts while you are fresh and rested. For each excuse you can find, try answering with a logical solution.

5. Implement a progress review routine.

That is crucial to reach success in a plan. Many people have heard that let's make a "backup plan" if these fail, mostly in action movies or tv shows. But this is not your case, and we are talking about your happiness, your success, etc., then; will your Plan B live almost happy or near success? I don't think so, right?

We want to reach our goals all the way, and what we need is hard work. Why? Because if you have set a goal and it is not inspiring you enough or your lack self-control.

All these aspects need to be set in writing to make the required adjustments in your project progress review. For example, you need to review your current daily schedule if you can't work on your tasks because you lack free time. We all have 24 hours. I'm sure you don't work 23 hours and 59 minutes every day, Monday thru Sunday, right?

You need to adjust and set priorities. "The purpose of a plan is to help you determine how best to achieve it."

How to set a goal

How to CHOOSE a goal?
Do you have problems choosing a goal?
Do you have too many?
Or don't you have any goals at all?

We all want a better life. We all have wishes. Wishes are goals - but goals with snap, crackle, and pop. Goals provide the process that can take you where you want to go, but too often, they don't inspire you. Wishes are different. They have an impact - like being struck by lightning instead of by a lightning bug. They let you dream. They let you soar. They allow you to tap into a source of limitless possibility and boundless energy that gives you the power to accomplish what you might otherwise never have imagined.

If you want to make things happen in your life, don't think about goals - think about making your wishes come true.

Before you can make your wishes come true, you must first decide what to wish for. Many people grind through one workweek after another, daydreaming about the good life. Nevertheless, they rarely master a clear idea of what that "good life" should be. Not what you're supposed to want, not what someone else wants for you, but what you in your heart want for yourself.

Are you willing to pay the PRICE?

At a cocktail party one evening, a famous pianist gave a recital. Afterward, her hostess said, "I would give anything to be able to play like you."

The pianist looked at her thoughtfully for a moment and replied, "No, you wouldn't."
The hostess, surprised and embarrassed in front of her guest, said, "I most certainly would." The pianist shook her head. "You would love to play as I play now, but you are not willing to practice eight hours a day for twenty years to learn how to play that way."

Take whatever you want,
said God, but pay for it.
- Spanish Proverb

Every wish has its price. You can have anything
you want if you are willing to pay that price. The
price may be time, money, or effort. It may be in
what you have to give up getting what you want.
Your willingness to pay the price is what gives you
the power to cause your wish to come true. If you
are 100% willing to pay the price, you are 100%
likely to succeed.
Pay the price, and your wish will come true.

How To Achieve A Goal

Step 1 - Intensify DESIRE

"Desire is the first step of goal achievement and
the foundation."

Have you set personal or business goals and failed
to achieve them?

Here is a crucial question: WHY?

The answer is simple: Because we did not have a strong enough desire.

Some may argue with that. "But I did have a strong desire, and still, I didn't get there." Sorry, but the desire was still not strong enough.

How do you identify intense desire and passion?

It's what keeps people working all hours, up early and late to bed. The "desire" dominates the conversation, thinking, and actions. Take a moment to think about the goals you've set for yourself. How committed are you to achieving these goals? Under what conditions would you give up?

What if you could significantly increase your desire to achieve these goals?

What if you wanted them so badly that you knew with absolute certainty that you would absolutely, positively never give up?

When you are truly 100% committed to reaching your goals, you move from hoping to knowing. If you want something badly enough, then quitting is simply not an option. You either find a way or make one. You pay the price, whatever it takes.

By creating intense desire, you can realize the impossible dream.

Develop a sincere desire to achieve the goal. A wish or daydream has no substance; it is vague, unformed, and unsupported by action. Desire puts effort into your plan. Strong desire is success power.

Step 2 - Develop BELIEF

If you don't believe you can reach a goal, it will remain a channel dream as if you didn't bother planning the route to the destination or do what's required to get there.

If you doubt that you may not be able to achieve something, you don't give it; you are all. You may very well just set it aside. In order to fully achieve anything, you must believe it is possible at a cellular level.

Believing is seeing. Seeing is believing.

If you are willing to accept that, you can be successful; you'll enjoy being successful. And suppose you are eager to establish and work on an exhilarating, enjoyable, and rewarding path to your goals. In that case, we're confident you'll reach those goals.

Step 3 - Define your OBJECTIVE

In May of 1961, John F. Kennedy pledged that America would land a man on the moon "before the decade is out." It was a brave and bold objective, perhaps one of the greatest of all time.

Just making the statement, however, did not lead to its achievement.

We define the Objective as the final goal. It is what all your efforts are going to lead to. In Investing, for example, it could be to have $1 million by retirement.

While some people may want only to have an Objective in one area of their life, most successful people set Objectives in many areas:

- Career

- Family
- Financial
- Health
- Knowledge
- Material Retirement
- Spiritual

These are just some categories you should set Objectives in. Objectives are generally long-term, sometimes even lifetime, although they don't have to be. They have to be important to you, something you feel is worth pursuing, or establishing a goal-setting routine wouldn't be worth doing.

In starting a goal-setting routine, we recommend you set Objectives in one or two areas to begin. As you start realizing small successes, you'll probably add more Objectives as you will want to succeed in all areas of your life.

Remember, don't hold back:

Make your Objectives as large as you can realistically realize. Make sure that your goals are S.M.A.R.T.!!! Commit to making SMART goals and start working toward them today.

Step 4 - WRITE it down!

Write your goal out in complete detail.

Why is it so important to write it down?

Words are an integral part of the thinking process. Words convey images, pictures, feelings, and emotions to the mind. That abstract thought now takes on body, shape, form, and substance by clothing it in words.

It is no longer just a thought!

It becomes something that motivates us or creates a gut feeling inside.

Why is the mechanical act of writing so important?

Building on what we have already stated, putting pen to paper now transfers those expressions which embody thoughts onto something tangible. We can now physically look at it. Even the act of using the eye in coordination with the hand holding the pen makes a much firmer impression on our mind as we write out the phrase or expression. When we read and re-read that phrase or sentence, the impression on the mind becomes deeper and deeper.

Written goals are directives to the unconscious mind, which obeys them blindly. There is something semi-magical about writing one's goals down, which makes achieving well-written goals an almost certainty. The real trick is to write one's goals down in a way that helps guarantee their achievement.

Please write it down or kiss it goodbye.

Step 5 - Set a DEADLINE

Set a date for the achievement of your goal.

Setting a date to attain your goal is the ignition for the goal-seeking missile in your mind. Make sure that your date is realistic... not too soon that it's impossible, but not so delayed that it's not interesting. Make sure you write the date of your goal down next to it. Once you've set this date, you should never change it.

Can we see then why dead lining is another crucial step in the goal achievement process?

Yes, deadlines crystallize thinking and increase motivation. However, it would be a mistake to think deadlines perform miracles.

Setting a deadline by saying, "In seven days from now, I will have made an extra $5,000," is not going to deliver miraculously. Unless you have a strategy and a realistic plan based on your present circumstances.

Set a deadline. Deadlines move us to action.

When we fail to include a deadline for our goal, when we commit to achieving it "as soon as possible," the goal winds up in our "as soon as possible" pile of things I will do another day, which is probably never. Why? Because we all have too much to do and not enough time to get, it all done. The items that have deadlines for completion tend to bubble up in priority and importance to take action and achieve them.

The journey of a thousand miles begins with a single step. No goal achievement is a leap across some vast canyon. Many are intimidated and driven away from going after what they want in their lives for fear they will have to take a giant leap across that canyon, and, hey, what if I don't leap far enough? Disaster.

But until you write out your goal, quantify it, and set a deadline, you break it down into small steps. It will forever appear to be too big a stretch and, therefore, unattainable. But every time you follow these three steps and break the goal down, you will always find that you have within your control what it takes to accomplish that next step. And once you begin, you are on your way!

Step 6 - Defining Your REASONS

In studying goal setting, the keys to success discovered that many people fail to achieve success simply because they lack clear REASONS.

Don't let this hold up your success. Consider why you want to achieve an Objective and write down what you've decided.

Do you want $1 or $2 million at retirement?
Why?
Do you say you want to live in a mansion?
Why?

The more compelling your Reasons are, the greater your chances will be of meeting your Objectives. Conversely, if you can't come up with "good" Reasons, you might as well set another Objective, as you won't achieve this one.

Remember, every person has different reasons for wanting something. What one person thinks is vain or stupid, another will think is worthy or great.

You must come up with Reasons that are honest, strong, and motivating to you.

Write them down below the appropriate Objective, leaving plenty of space to expand or add to them: the more Reasons you have, the better. Just make sure they really represent the Reasons you have for desiring something.

Step 7- Defining Your SUB-GOALS

Once you've written an Objective and your compelling Reasons for achieving it, you must start planning the route toward the Objective.

Ask yourself: "What steps do I need to take to.............?"
These steps will be your Subgoals.

Say you've set an Objective of having $1 Million by retirement (which could be 20+ years away). First, you must figure out how you can achieve that.
Do you need to learn more about investing?
Will you have to start saving $500 or $250 a week?
Do you have to get a new job?
Will you have to watch your existing investments more actively?
Whatever needs doing to progress towards your Objective will become your Sub-goals.
Subgoals can be specific or broad in scope, but they must always lead directly toward the Objective they support. They must also always have a deadline. A date you plan to accomplish the Sub-goal by, a realistic date that motivates you into action and ensures progress towards your Objective.

Usually, you will have many Sub-goals at a time. In the case of a sincere long-term Objective, some of the Subgoals will not be clear at the start, with others coming about when certain existing Subgoals are achieved.

Always write your Subgoals and their Accomplishment Dates down. Never make your Subgoals too long or too difficult, as you don't want to be overwhelmed by them. If a Subgoal is long-term (as in taking a four-year degree towards a larger Career Objective), break it down into smaller parts (each year, for example) and revise and, or renew them when accomplished.

By making sufficient and reasonable Sub-goals and always accomplishing them on time, you'll find yourself making significant progress toward Objectives. Which may look intimidating, or even impossible, by themselves.

Step 8- Defining Your TASKS

Just as we break large or long-term Objectives into smaller supporting elements called Sub- goals, we further break our Sub-goals into even smaller pieces. These small elements are called Tasks and accomplishing them makes the practice of goal setting really work.

Tasks are usually the simple things you must do to accomplish a Subgoal. Suppose you've set a Sub-goal, for example, to completely understand investing in bonds by next June 15th. In that case, you will have to accomplish several Tasks to acquire that knowledge.

Going to the library and getting a book on bonds would be a Task.

Reading the book for one hour each this Monday, Wednesday, and Friday could be three separate Tasks.

Visiting Investors Skills' website for their bond information would be another Task. Calling your buddy who's had success in the bond market would also be a task.

These tasks, which should be written on the same paper as the Sub-goal they support, must be set with an Accomplishment Date. If you procrastinate calling your buddy, never thoroughly read the book, or don't even bother checking the website. You won't reach your Sub-goal of learning about bonds or won't meet it by its Accomplishment Date.

And this, unfortunately for you, will turn your $1 Million retirement Objective back into the pipe dream it didn't have to be.

By focusing your mind on the easy-to-accomplish Tasks and completing those tasks, you'll be making significant progress toward your Subgoals and Objectives without feeling overwhelmed. Make sure to write down ALL Tasks, even those that take only minutes to complete. Then, when they're accomplished, check them off.

As more and more Tasks are successfully accomplished and checked off, you'll find yourself becoming more encouraged and more confident about your abilities. The more you believe, the more you will strive to accomplish, and you will enjoy completing even more Tasks. And the more Tasks you complete on time, the closer you'll be to that success. You have real Reasons for wanting— the success you originally defined as your Objectives.

The power of the FIRST STEP

Do you know the essential secret of goal setting? No? So what are you waiting for?

Personal and Business Goals

That is one classic example of "goal-setting." That means lots of work and possibly getting yourself at risk, which involves fear and doubt, such as getting indebted, losing your assets, a lawsuit, etc. We must divide our personal and business goals because you will inevitably make money if you want to succeed. If this is not your intention, your plan will be different. Why? Allow me to explain:

When you build a business plan, you have several blocks to construct an organized blueprint. You work on marketing, service or product line, funding, and financials, which are money. If you are making a non-profit organization, work on your numbers. The difference is the profit they reinvest in the non-profit projects. In regular business, profit is earned by the owner(s).

That is very simple and logical; you have specific money goals to meet. At the very least, you need to pay your lease, power, water, Internet, and phone bill. You have twenty-two working days each month, adding up all expenses and dividing them by twenty-two. You have the value in the currency you live on how much money you need to make each working day to cover your monthly costs.

You need to write and calculate how much money you will need to sustain your operation until the cash comes in in your business plan. Otherwise, you will be out of business. That is why many companies require a financial injection. It could be a bank loan, an investor, or many other alternatives.

Based on your marketing projections, your business will need at least six months of capital to cover the initial expenses. They should use any income coming in to gain liquid money, not to pay their initial investment. You can do this when you have a constant flow according to your financial plan.

If you have a business and numbers are not met. Maybe you are confused about what your company should do to generate revenue, meaning you have weak "Sales." You need to pay attention and do the work.

Another cause could be your market analysis and marketing strategy. In this case, you need to go out and talk to your customers to find out if they fit your product or service and readjust all your plan to keep your business afloat.

An alternative cause could be that you have not set a salary for yourself in your business. You are taking money from your company, affecting your operation and the financials. Suppose you have skipped this part of your plan. Stop all daily activities and add at least a basic salary covering all your simple expenses. No luxuries of any kind, just the essentials; readjust your budget and move forward.

If you haven't read Robert Kiyosaki's book, Rich Dad's Cashflow Quadrant is good reading. In the book, he talks about what we try to achieve with a business: building a system working for us and being a business owner. In his quadrant, it shows: "an Employee has a job," "a self-employed owns a job," "a business owner owns a system," and last, "the investor money works for you."

On which side of the quadrant do you want to be?

That is a tricky question you need to answer right away. It will help you determine which side of the quadrant you want to be and the pathway you want to take, and there are four directions; Decide and leave your fear and move on!

Once you have your mindset and decide you have made a choice, you have overcome the fear of indecision. Then now, you can reduce your fear, keep learning how to maintain your self-control, and continue learning new skills.
But if you feel you have imagined as a business something different and it is not meeting your expectations. Perhaps you have found a hobby or a noble cause you can help with. Then your focus needs to change, and either you find a job to support you or keep searching until you find a business idea that combines your two passions.

I have met many individuals who love to have a business. Very talented and disciplined people whom you feel they would do great are business owners. Still, they haven't found a way to put an idea together and launch a business. That was my inspiration to write the book "Being Broke No More, Overcome the rat race and establish abundant living" (BBNM). The purpose of that book is to contribute insights about starting a business with low risk. You can join the Service-based business by selling your knowledge and skills. In that way, you can start having additional funding for your project, startup, or side hustle idea. Again, all you need is your willpower to make it happen!

I remember having a controversy with the first title of BBNM because I wanted to name my book "Become an entrepreneur while you are still at your job, key steps to start a business with no risk." Everybody stated you would have a risk in many businesses. It doesn't matter in what field it would be; if you leave that title, you will cheat readers about the book. When you become numb to the risk and have controlled your fear of failing, jumping on new startups, partnerships, and more is straightforward.

There are many million-dollar ideas, but they will stay that way if you don't act. If you feel you have an idea that solves people's pain, you would be close to having a business if you feel insecure (afraid to fail). You can visit my website and find resources to help you https://eliacevedo.com/programs/. Look for Business Start Up Program and click if the program is open. I normally open this program two or three times a year. If you find it closed, please subscribe to the waiting list.

Many people are doing very well today. They are pleased with their comfort zone while having a good-paying job and a level of stability, allowing them to live happy lives. Having a business is not on their radar. In this scenario, there are a few things that can occur. One of them is one of your friends or coworkers who wants to invite you to join their business idea, leaving your security and stability behind to pursue a dream. The other one is that your world got rocked, and your stability has a massive earthquake. It would be best if you reacted and did anything to keep everything spinning; you are forced to leap.

Understandably, few people got what it takes to be an entrepreneur or to build a business. However, we will never know what will happen if you have made that move.

I just can't stand people being unhappy doing the same job and complaining for years. If you want to stay there until retirement age, I'm okay with it. Find a job you enjoy doing and pay you good money to sustain a decent lifestyle.

With the Pandemic, I believe we are all in for a major challenge. COVID-19 has resulted in the loss of many employments, the closure of enterprises, and heightened economic uncertainty. Many people are struggling to make ends meet these days as a result of lower wages or unemployment. Yet not everything is negative since when we confront problems, we all want to succeed and move forward. To manage their money throughout the pandemic, many people used budgeting tactics such as cutting back on costs. Others turned to remote employment to keep companies running and money sources flowing.

To provide financial assistance to individuals and businesses affected by the pandemic, the United States government sponsored numerous stimulus packages, including the CARES Act. Direct payments to individuals, extended unemployment compensation, and loans and incentives for small enterprises were all included.

Some people used the pandemic to engage in the stock market or other investment vehicles to produce cash, while others used it to gain new skills or pursue education to improve their employability and income potential.

I know those were difficult times, but we worked hard to overcome them, and most people have changed. If you still have reservations about your ability to succeed. Remember what we all went through a few years ago? I understand that most people forget the past and focus on the present, but if you want to change your current reality, you can't stay where you are.

Afraid of Money

That is a very common misconception. On many occasions, we are told directly or indirectly that having lots of money is a sin, A bad thing, and many more. I have built a list that I want to share with you:

- Money makes people greedy.
- Money is the root of all evil.
- I'm not good with money.
- My family has never been rich.
- Money is a limited resource.
- Work your *ss off to get wealthy.
- You can be rich or happy.
- Wanting lots of money is selfish.

If you identify with any of those sentences listed, you need to change your relationship with money. You need to understand that "money is a currency" in any part of the globe. Money doesn't care if you are happy or sad. Your last bill is before you fall bankrupt if it gets dirty or if it gets old.

Money never gets emotional. And should not be such a significant thing in our life that it can decree our emotional state or determine our self-worth. Think about that. Save and store this in your mind. "Money is a tool that results from your fortune." For example, if you solve a pain or a significant problem for people, guess what. You will make lots of money, and folks will be thankful for your idea while giving you, their money.

It's a matter of focus; you may make lots of money. Many people think that if they offer a service that helps another individual, they should give it for free, but this is not true. That is not how the economy works.

I can share the feeling of making lots of money; It's not compared, such as having extra bucks in a paycheck, really changing your life. How you wake up every day, your present and plans, the destinations you want to visit, and the future for your family and relatives. The feeling is inexplicably good; You feel weightless and free. But it also comes with a responsibility; you need to pay attention to your money and not treat it like a "person," you just need to learn how to appreciate it.

Quit denying that money is essential in life. In today's economy, money is essential; You want housing, food, clothes, and healthcare, right? If you're going to help, a relative or any person close to you will need the money if they are struggling. You can help. That doesn't mean that you will solve money problems for everyone. You can apply logic if you want to help someone: "Give a Man a Fish, and You Feed Him for a Day; Teach a Man to Fish, and You Feed Him for a Lifetime.

What does this mean? It means you will provide support in the "short term." And help them develop a plan to support themselves and get the education required in areas where you have assessed they have flaws. Nobody will force you if you don't want to do it, but it will be wise to watch Schindler's List to give you another perspective.

Now let's think about making lots of money. How you can change your present, let's set a target big enough that makes you nervous but generates excitement, build a plan to make it real, use your logic, and put it into practice.

You want to make $100,000 or 1 million dollars. Here you will find some logic that you apply to your plan and reach your targeted figure:

$100,000 requires 10 clients to pay $10,000 dollars.
$100,000 requires 20 clients to pay $5,000 dollars.
$100,000 requires 30 clients to pay $3,334 dollars.
$100,000 requires 40 clients to pay $2,500 dollars.
$100,000 requires 75 clients to pay $1,334 dollars.
$100,000 requires 100 clients to pay $1,000 dollars.
$100,000 requires 500 clients to pay $200 dollars.
$100,000 requires 5,000 clients to pay $20 dollars.

You need to do a basic calculation to determine how many people per month you need to reach in a year to fulfill your commitment and make your 100k goal. Let's say to make 100k with a product or service at the rate of 200 dollars; this means you need to reach 500 clients to achieve your goal.

The next step is finding how many monthly sales you must make, and then you take 100k, divided by 12 months. The result will give you several clients equal to 41.6667, let's say 42 clients per month. We have about twenty-two working days each month, so we have to divide the number of clients by the number of days available again. The result is 1.909090. Let's round up to two clients per day.

You have 480 minutes in eight hours to find two people to purchase your product or service. You can spend four hours convincing one person. I think you can do better than that, don't you?

If you can't, you don't have to worry about it. Many entrepreneurs hate sales. Afraid of being rejected by a customer or afraid to convince someone about the pain you are solving. There is a logical solution for using a person with the sales skill you demand. Your net achievement of 100k will be affected by that new person's expense, and that's okay; you should build up a team.

Think about our modern economy; Today, we don't have limitations per city, county, state, or country; we are in a global society with around 7.x billion or close to 8 billion people. Just imagine if you solve a problem affecting 5% of the worldwide population. You charge them 1 dollar, and you will reach $350.000.000 million.

As you can see, numbers don't get excited or moody. They think of a way to make money. Just apply some ethics and logic to your business practice. You will be a significant contribution to our society.

When you are about to launch your business, you should consider having or building a team and a network of providers soon. That will allow you to have more free time. You are free to choose where to invest your time, whether within your business or your family, or perhaps both; balance is the key.

You need to learn something fundamental about yourself: how to act when you have lots of money and when you don't have any money. It would be best if you were yourself; Learn to control your ego and maintain yourself in a position where all your beliefs stay together. It's very common for new millionaires to go bankrupt in the next five years. That is because they spend more of what they earn, and when you have lots of excesses, the effects won't look promising.

Keep your feet on the ground and find a healthy group to hang out with to become a better person each day. Read tons of books, go out and dance, connect to a yoga club, join a cause, and use your wealth and energy for something good. It doesn't have to be in another country; narrow it down as close to your family members, community, etc.

Having a team will eventually become a family. Your team members will reveal their skills, and you will trust them to carry your message while your business is growing. For many entrepreneurs and existing business owners, letting go is one of the most complex parts. They want to control every single aspect of the business. In the end, they affect productivity because they could be an obstacle for that team member.

I love to share Bill Gates' story with Microsoft. He is a brilliant man. He knew if he didn't take care of his people, those supporting his company on the back end would eventually not have a business. His main priority had enough funding for his team, and his goal was to have one full year of financial backup. He will not have to face laying off team members if something happens on the market. No wonder he got about 18 years on the world's billionaires list.

Instead of being afraid to be helpful in your business, you must let go. You can build a process and share your knowledge and experience with every team member. And make room for improvement; you never know what that new pupil will contribute to your business. And you can refer to a great team such as the Disney brothers, Walt, and Roy. Walt was the creative mind of all those beautiful characters we grew. Still, Roy was the master builder. He oversaw the operation of what we today known as the Disney Empire.

I don't know about you, but if it does not motivate you to make money right away, I don't know what it would be. Come on, let's get moving!

Chapter 2

"Always remember that you are absolutely unique.
Just like everyone else."
-Margaret Mead

Why do you wish to make a change?

This is the most crucial question because we are
always looking for rewards in anything we do.
We've been trained in this manner since we were
children, at home, school, college, and even at
work. Many more questions occur due to the basis,
end goal, or desire to modify anything. It is usually
our motivation. For example, in my earlier book,
"Being Broke No More," the primary purpose is to
pull yourself out of the rat race. And if you're
unfamiliar with the term, I'll explain it briefly.

You work hard, put in your hours, and endure your
workplace atmosphere, management, board of
directors, or anyone that hammers your existence

daily. But it appears that no matter what you do, you are stuck. Your earnings need to be consistently increased. It appears challenging to flourish since something happens just when you think you are ready to move forward. You're trying to save money, and certain outside forces are aware of it because it's always needed. Things usually work out; you can keep and lower your credit card debt, but your world has been rocked again, and we must start over.

The rat race is an analogy for running your buttocks off for a small return. With that said, the obvious next step is to alter your current reality. You may be wondering how to do this, and there is only one viable answer: DECIDE.

We discussed fear and its various manifestations in the last chapter. You cannot change or aim to seek change until you are willing to decide and begin controlling your anxieties.

You're looking for a solution, but you'll have to do it on your own.

I know what you're thinking: Why would I be reading this book if I knew the solution? And, in case you missed it, I said it on the previous page. It would be best to determine whether you wish to change.

Assume you wish to improve your relationship with your spouse or a family member. In that situation, certain aspects make you uneasy. You must take the initial step, and if your desire is genuine, you will not stop until you achieve your goal.

To effect CHANGE, you must DECIDE, devise a strategy to overcome or deal with those problems, and ACT ON IT.

Setting the instructions is the first step you take after deciding to change. That means you must take the following five steps:

Step one: Make an excuse cheat sheet.
Step two: Is to write down your strategy.
Step three: Create a goal-achieving routine.
Step four: Keep track of your progress.
Step five: Make a plan for failing or not committing.

Step one: Make an excuse cheat sheet.

We are unwilling to change under normal circumstances since many things and ties are attached to our justifications. Your fundamental challenge is why we are unable to fulfill any obligation.
But we may avoid defeat by knowing and preparing for it. Because humans are emotionally

oriented and reasoning is typically beaten, we can design a mind-focused method and eliminate mental disputes.

You must be honest and write down why you believe you will never be able to attain X or Y in your life. When working with excellent clients or achieving great things, we all get distracted by shiny object syndrome. And that's okay since it's something written in our DNA. But we need to keep our plan close to hand to prevent becoming distracted and losing our bearings. We can't stop responding to stimuli, but the key is to be prepared and recover swiftly.

People leave a seminar, webinar, or other motivational event inspired, pumped, and excited because they have purchased the "What's in it for me?" They are offering a new promise, a new way that, in many circumstances, has the potential to last. However, as the days pass, the majority will gradually return to the same old pattern.

Writing about oneself is one of the most difficult things to do. When questioned, we frequently discuss what we have studied, the type of work we do, or our academic abilities. And, while you may believe that you are simply humble, the truth is that we are afraid to reveal any personal information.

To capitalize on our proclivity for novelty, we must first learn to recognize it. We must learn to use our novelty center because our brain is only stimulated when we discover something new. We are prone to succumbing to temptation with each new technology, piece of clothing, etc. And this is the number one reason we start some tasks and never finish them: it does not produce additional newness. It appears to be tedious and even an additional effort or chore.

When we start learning about ourselves and how to deal with our natural tendencies, our plans become easier to implement because we already know how we might react. And it will allow us to conquer and progress to the next step.

Step two: Is to write down your strategy.

A plan is a useful tool since it directs you in the right way. If you have written step one, it is obvious that you have already registered what you do not want for your immediate future. It would be beneficial if you infused dopamine into your strategy, which would assist your brain in viewing your plan as a novelty, a new chance, and receiving the ultimate reward.

Assume you aren't sure what you want out of life yet, but whatever is going on in your life. We all want to be healthy and wealthy so that we can do whatever we want. We shall continue to live a limitless lifestyle. If you have the thinking, "Well, this looks good, but I don't see myself doing it." This is the precise moment when your excuses cheat sheet will come in handy. You are dealing with a limiting belief and must have a defense mechanism to proceed. Keep your step one sheet close at hand.

When developing our strategy, we must learn, grasp, and perfect the "WIIFM" or "What's in it for me" method. Because you must purchase this plan for the sake of your life and those around you; else, this will be just another attempt.

You will need input on the following aspects to construct this plan:

- Examine your harmful or unhealthy habits.
- Make yourself responsible for changing your habits.
- Eliminate negative triggers.
- Believe in your abilities.
- Recognize setbacks

I hope this example inspires you to begin your new goal-change journey. During this procedure, it is critical to synchronize your thoughts and beliefs because they will play a prominent role. The irony is that they will play the devil's card because if your beliefs are positive, you will progress and achieve your goal. Assume, however, that they are the antagonist in your life. Those ideas will hold you back, and any progress you make will be washed away because it was insufficient.

You already know this; give up now. Stop wasting time; let us keep things cool and move forward. Step one is essential because we must become mentally healthy and strong enough to overcome the worries that our beliefs have planted.

We should go to the gym to work out our bodies, but we should also work out our thoughts. Because the media, news, the Internet, and our culture are rife with toxic and deceptive messages that might prey on one of our vulnerabilities and plant a false notion.

If you want to develop a strong mindset, you must discover a group of people who share or have a better mindset than you. Don't be concerned if you feel vulnerable at first. As you begin to exercise your mind, new problems will present themselves, and you will be prepared to deal with any situation. Remember that some problems are for robots, software, and mathematics, while others are for humans.

In my specific circumstance, I have numerous plans that last from 42 and 90 days. After that period, initiatives are revisited for evaluation and reinforcement, indicating if we are on track to meet our objectives or are falling short.

To assist you in clarifying. Each milestone timeline is 42 days if I pursue a long-term objective. Remember that this is a long-term endeavor; defining deadlines is critical because demonstrated time frames can aid. For example, if you want to form a new habit, you must practice it for 21 or 22 days. And if you want that habit to become a habit, you must commit to it for 90 days. It would be beneficial if you considered why I give a specified number of days to do this task. You need deadlines and dedication to get things done if you want to develop self-control; otherwise, you will waste your time.

During this first stage, you must identify your distractions. And keep them from becoming the focal point of your job or focusing on self-rewards such as video games or excessive online time.

I've developed a time management method, and an eBook and a course will be available soon. It facilitates a procedure where you can work a few hours daily and accomplish the same amount as you would during an 8-hour workday.

This process is aided by a focus on efficacy rather than productivity. When working on a given activity, you must offer more than 100 percent of yourself because the end goal is to complete it. You can appear busy and do only what is necessary. Your workdays and goal-setting will be forever altered as soon as you realize this.

Step three: Create a goal-achieving routine.

This phase is critical for creating goal-driven routines since it requires action. You are not Aladdin and do not have a genie to assist you. If one of your goals is to lose 10 pounds, you must exercise for a certain amount of time to cause your organism to burn the calories and energy needed to achieve your goal. Your diet is also interesting and should be incorporated into this new habit.

Having said that, watching videos of people exercising or eating healthy will only suffice if you watch them learn about your upcoming routine in making healthy meals and the type of activities for each muscle region. You don't have to go to the gym and let your credit card do it for you. You may readily locate high-intensity interval training (HIIT) regimens on YouTube. This interval training is a little difficult for beginners, but there is just too much information on fitness for you only to complete it if that is your aim.

I'm not sure if it's appropriate for you. However, in order to carry out your plan, you must consider and keep all previous actions on hand. You will be tempted to revert to your old habits until you perfect them.

A To-Do list is one tool that can assist you in mastering goal-driven routines. The To-Do list alone will not serve since you will need follow-up and regular reminders to check, reorganize, appraise, and get to it.

Another consideration is the word "routine." Some people object to structure because they believe it limits their creativity. And let me tell you, that is not the case.

For instance, suppose you are a creative individual who works on promotional materials. To let your imagination run wild, you'll need some context to understand your client's requirements and develop the components accordingly. That means your creative process requires a foundation before your ideas can flow.

You must also conduct research to understand your client's competition and target audience. During this time, your concept takes shape in your mind. You start drawing or composing bullet points when you think you've got anything. Then you move on with all of those sketches and let the creative process flow since you can't take forever to do this because your client has given you a deadline. You and your organization are determined to succeed. Remember that ideas are only the beginning; they will only be completely developed if you work on them, develop them, and put them into action.

This may be referred to as a process, structure, or routine, but whatever happens in between, tasks must be completed, and you must care for yourself or your family.

There are various types of To-Do lists, but all of them exist to assist you in getting things done; here are a few examples:

- Personal
- Work
- Commute
- Family
- Chores
- Shopping list
- Someday

Many novices need to improve with the to-do list method because they believe everything must be completed in one day. This strategy helps you focus your day, and it is not a strict schedule that you must follow, or you will fail.

Your To-Do list will help you prioritize your day by emphasizing the most critical tasks for today. Because you worked on your list the day before, you can schedule commuting times if you need to see a doctor or get papers.

For example, the following To-Do list can assist you in developing your morning routine:

Personal To-Do List

- Wake up at 5:00 am
- Drink water and do Yoga or HIIT for 15 minutes
- Fix your bed
- Order your room
- Take a shower and get ready
- Have breakfast

That list can be completed in one hour; by 6:00 a.m., you are already a winner because your duties are completed. This list, of course, can be tailored to your specific requirements. The most crucial benefit is that it will assist you in developing a morning habit.

A few years ago, my morning to-do list was:

- Wake up at 5:00 am
- Read 15 minutes

- Write 15 minutes
- 10-min home workout
- Shower
- Get dressed and ready

You now have a reason to get out of bed, a victory for you right at the start of the day. When you start your day with a win, your commute will be more enjoyable, and you can then start adding components that will give you more motivation to achieve your goals.

Many individuals listen to podcasts instead of listening to the news while commuting. You must watch the news in order to know how the traffic is. However, modern vehicles and mobile applications feature a navigation tool that allows you to get input on what is happening on the road from other drivers. Using this existing resource, you escape the temptation of feeding your mind with the worry that the daily news channel brings.

If you have a long commute, make a list of it. Instead of being frustrated by the long travel, you might use that crucial time to establish your priorities. And you're listening to podcasts to help you progress and grow.

Step four: Keep track of your progress.

First and foremost, remember that you are not in school and will make mistakes, miss deadlines, and even get things incorrect at first. Measuring your development is beneficial since it allows you to analyze and assess how well you are doing and what changes you should make.

As a result, it is critical to establish time frames because it enables you to evaluate and correct actions that are not being prioritized and have been moved in their sequence for whatever reason. For example, suppose you began your day at 5:00 a.m. You take out your phone, switch off the alarm, and go straight to any social media outlet. Your day has changed in less time than you realize, for 30 minutes have passed, and you have no idea how it happened. I've been there; it's not like I've never explored.

The most crucial component of this tracking process recognizes that we must learn to regulate it. In addition, an algorithm targets us on each platform, and it knows about us and what we look for and want. Its objective is to enhance our viewing time so platforms can profit from it. Because you think in a different way as you learn to track your progress, you will become more efficient with your time and more selective in the types of actions you engage in. You will concentrate your thoughts on your objectives and the steps you must take to achieve them.

Step five: Make a plan for failing or not committing.

This stage of the process involves reviewing how you are doing with your plan, determining which areas need improvement and which require assistance, and checking on what is going on. That is obtained in step four.

By no means, though, am I making an apology to you. "Oh no! The algorithm is so strong that I can't go off social media." I'm preparing you for the fact that your plan will have to cope with algorithms and people who like to gossip and distractions that are all over the place.

Another word of caution: you must let go of self-punishment. We don't need that here; you certainly won't bring it into the mix. You're learning, and it's okay to make mistakes, but you can't stay in this cycle once you've realized you've failed. If you still need to complete a task and it is nearing completion, you don't have to start crying, blaming yourself for your views, and engaging in self-sabotage.

The correct goal is to fix items or behaviors that are not beneficial to the broader process. Please recognize that this is a learning experience and that this is our first time embracing it in our lives. But, from now on, each mistake we have uncovered that is not assisting us in carrying out our plan must be confronted, discussed, and remedied since your strategy will not change.

I wouldn't say I like hearing individuals discuss "plan B," which is not an option when working on your goal. That is already abandoning your principal plan. If you already have a B plan in place, write it down.

I intend to live a healthy lifestyle in order to live a long life and be able to support my children. What is your take on having a backup plan?

- I'd like to purchase the car of my dreams. Plan B will be to purchase my friend's dream car?
- I'm looking for my soul mate... Plan B will be...
- I want to be happy... Plan B will be...

The question will arise: Are you sticking with the success of your plan, or are you considering a backup plan?

Using fear as motivation

In Chapter One, we talk about fear; if we don't control it, it can go out of our control, limiting our lives. As we age, we learn from our friends, family members, and peers that, in many cases, we need the motivation to get going. However, sometimes we lack the will, and potent fear-based motivators put us into action.

If you were in college and not paying attention, you were a candidate for a pop question or standing in front of your class and rehearsing what your teacher said. The motivation was aimed at getting attention so that you would learn today's lesson. And as we progress in life, we are thrown lots of fear-based motivators. For example, you need to run the extra mile to have your GPA in good standing to be accepted to college. Then when you present your admission test and know that this opportunity is a life changer, you fear not getting the expected results. You increase your chances by studying even harder.

The same happens at work because you are not doing your best. You know it, every time you are called to a meeting or have a phone from your boss, you get cold and sweaty hands because you are afraid that they will tell you that you are fired in that phone call or meeting because of your low performance or even a tiny mistake.

It would be best to reframe those thoughts because you feed the monster again. You don't need to worry if you are clear about what you are doing with your performance at work, in college, at home, or with your spouse. However, if you need to talk about anything related to fear, do so; don't let them set root and grow.

If you bury your fears, they will consume you to avoid having a setback during this new process, and it's essential to acknowledge them and talk about them with someone. You can take a few steps to turn fear into a motivator. It may not apply to many cases, but in terms of work and studies, I think that it helps a lot.

Breathe: Your mind is a thought highway, and breathing will help your mind ease and calm your body. Remember that most people tell us to breathe and count until ten. Later, you can do a breathing meditation for two to five minutes to help you clear your mind.

Mind your thoughts: You must start caring about what you think. We often have off-scope ideas that we even ask ourselves what we were thinking. And a very important also is paying attention to how you have felt. Suppose you cannot eat chocolate, but your mind focuses on the reward. It will trigger an action in no time, but you can talk to yourself and stop the incoming action if you have a response plan.

Rethink: Sometimes, we can talk mentally to ourselves, but if you have not yet learned to manage your fear, it will be hard to put things in perspective.

Remember that you are not in danger; also, you understand how your body reacts when its fear is triggered. Sweaty hands, stomachache, and several others will kick in, and by rethinking what will happen and the outcome, you can ease those thoughts.

Review and Assess: To clarify things, remember that when you experience fear, you receive a message. We are sensorial beings, and we react to anything naturally. Many situations may make us feel uncomfortable, and we try as much as we can to avoid any pain. Review what is happening and check if it's worth being afraid of that.

Move: Now that you have a small process to use fear as a motivator, and it's time to cut the talk and get into action. Remember that fear works both ways as an action stopper or fuel to propel you to move forward.

Our lives are filled with challenges and obstacles, and it is crucial to live our life full of self-realization and joy. You can take control of your life and take it to the level you want; nothing stops you.

Over the entire book, we have talked about options and steps for reaching your destined glory, but there is no way you can do that only by reading a book; you need to act. It would be best to say out loud that you want to change and are committed to it. If you are ready to go, visit my website and get the 30-day challenge here https://eliacevedo.com/books/the-invisible-chain/.

Well, you got this. We have talked about Chapter one. If you are still unsure how to deal with it, I invite you to return to chapter one and domestic your fear monster.

Remember that we cannot remove fear. It's a built-in mechanism, and you just need to learn how to make it work in your favor. When creating your plan, you should feel a little fear because you will be stretching your capabilities to achieve things in life.
Remember, you can use fear to face every situation or run away, forgetting everything you have worked for. Fear can be understood as a fuel to propel you or an anchor that will hold you back. It's just a matter of choice.

What Exactly Is Mindset?

I'm not sure how many of you understand what mindset is. If you're still not sure, remember that I shared the groundwork above, and if you need to go back and reread it, please do so before continuing with this chapter.

It is also critical to incorporate awareness in this definition because, in the end, your mindfulness will collaborate with your thoughts.

What is Mindfulness?

Being aware is closely tied to having a positive mindset. Both are inextricably related since your set of beliefs (mindset) will trigger your thoughts, causing your attention to be drawn to your senses, environment, and feelings.

Our thinking is at the heart of what we do, for whom we do it, and why. Your thinking will enable you to maintain a continuous focus on what you desire in life. However, if such an attitude is not developed, we will frequently base our decision on previous knowledge or experiences. That is both good and terrible since wisdom/knowledge may be a great asset in life, but incorrect knowledge can trap you in a cycle of ignorance.

As a result, both are inextricably linked to your fixed or development attitude. You must comprehend and devise ideas and techniques to assist you in shifting away from your concentrated thinking. And have all of the tools you need to create the new beliefs that will replace your old ones and set you on a new path.

The fixed or growth mindset can help you read and understand those around you throughout time. Since they are upbeat, you will eventually begin associating with folks with a growth attitude. Sharing experiences and embracing failing, flaws, and mistakes will provide you with motivational and energetic feelings. We all face setbacks as part of our lives, and they help us recall where we failed and learn our lesson.

You will feel encouraged and driven to go the additional mile if you find this environment since they think work and practice will lead to mastery. After all, socializing with people who have a high IQ will push you to keep progressing. Most of the time, you will be inspired at first, but in no time, you will share your accomplishment and inspire others to follow your path.

In other words, this mindset will see failures as a part of the learning process that will fuel and empower you to achieve your goals.

People who have a fixed mindset feel that talent and intelligence are fixed. It's easy to identify because there will be resistance when difficulties are provided because they are terrified of failing, which would be a showstopper.

People with a fixed attitude tend to freeze because they will not shift from their position. When you try to deliver nice comments, they will interpret it as a personal assault, while your constructive criticism will be ignored. Comparing people is a common offense since it is perceived as a threat. Most of the time, they will give up quickly because everyone else has a higher, impossible ideal.

But don't panic; assistance is available if you have fixed thinking. As previously said, your brain's adaptability will enable you to do so. This is the first step: believing your mindset can be altered, reframed, or educated from your current beliefs. Your internal monologue must shift from a judge type to a growth type.

Listen to your fixed mentality thoughts: When your "what ifs" and uncertainties arise, you must stop them from fading that concept. You'll need your contingency plan available during this initial process since you'll need to modify your attitude toward those events. I know it appears complicated, but it is similar to the first time you went to the gym; the first few days are painful, but everything begins to fall into place after a while.

Please understand that you have a choice: Everything in your life is up to you to determine how to handle it. Our lives are full of obstacles, disappointments, and criticism. You must decide whether or not to use them as fuel. Don't let your negative ideas take over; instead, quiet your inner voice that says, "What if..."

Answer with your growth mindset: I consulted with various experts. They confirmed that we have a small voice that speaks to ourselves and reads loudly when we read books. Or perhaps when we are alone. That small voice is our subconscious mind, sometimes known as our gut. That little voice is a representation of the angel and the evil talking with us, advising us on how to continue. The most important thing is to maintain a happy attitude; having our cheat sheet will help us in dealing with our ideas. If you are still unsure, consider the following examples:

What if you fail? You will say that failure is a necessary part of the learning process and that successful people experience it along the road.

Are you certain you can pull it off? You will respond, "I'm not sure I can do it right now, but I can learn with time and practice."

If I had the ability, it would be a piece of cake. We were born with no skills, and they are all reachable with dedication and a lot of effort.

For your growth attitude, use active voice: Your small voice demands action. That will become your primary option with practice and consistency.

Keep in mind that you can evolve into the next version of yourself and what you require. It's a basic system to follow, nothing too dramatic or drastic, but it requires a lot of hard effort and consistency. Would you like to give it a shot?

Limiting Beliefs & Objections

Things are finally aligning for me to begin deliberately addressing inquiries. Because we now understand that our mindset is linked to our beliefs, and we act or behave in accordance with our mindfulness. We must go back and analyze our beliefs, bring them into the present, and then understand how we feel.

We would begin to feel the energy associated with the type of belief that we are evoking. Allow me to elaborate.

I recently watched a seminar about neuroscience and how we can alter or train our brains. The metaphor used by the expert to describe the subject makes a lot of sense.

I'll employ a standard paradigm for computer file management in which the hard drive serves as the entire unit, "the brain." And our memories will be referred to as folders.

```
            / Folder 1
Hard drive – Folder 2
            \ Folder 3

            / Memory 1
Your Brain – Memory 2
            \ Memory 3
```

We will have millions of memories stored with that reference today. The trick is to refer to one of those folders whenever we mention one of our beliefs.

Another important factor is that we tend to keep memories based on how we recall them. For example, we have all had experiences we have saved and captured piece by piece, capturing the moment we want to last forever. Another type of compressed memory is an all-in-one memory, which does not have discrete portions.

With it as a foundation, I'll get to the point. We have memories loaded with various experiences that feed our thinking, whether fixed or growing, defining how our days will pass. It's fascinating because every time we pull or call a memory, our brain recreates the experience, much like watching a movie.

Our brain stores memories of current feelings and experiences, and we have nearly the same experience as we do now. I believe you are already aware of this.

The most shocking aspect is that whenever you make a change to that memory, your memory gets overwritten with the most recent alterations. We must go through a rational learning process to shift our ideas about particular things and events in our lives. And, if you have a plan or strategy for dealing with your memories, you can override those sensations and begin the process of healing or moving ahead.
The scientific term for this is neuroplasticity, which is the brain's ability to form and restructure experiences or responses.

As a result, my friend, you can change your beliefs in order to acquire a positive mindset. It would be ideal if you possessed the means to break free from the limitations that have plagued you for years and decide your future. One odd aspect of my writing on this subject, and the reason for the publication of this book, is that I am not an expert. But, throughout my journey, I frequently encountered people who were insecure. I wanted to address this issue thoroughly because it is, in some ways, the primary reason why some businesses and partnerships fail.

One or more business owners are referred to be "people" because they prioritize their agenda over the collaborative effort to name their business partnership. We've had to separate ourselves from CEOs and presidents in order to move forward and not listen to X or Y people who weren't understanding it. We've also discovered some fantastic people working for organizations with great ideas but are too hesitant to take risks and engage any company.

Returning to our brain and memory, the finding I learned from that movie truly affects how I think and will think about my beliefs from that point forward. You may need to fully comprehend how this works and how you can use it to your advantage. This is a personal journey that we must all begin.

I've also begun the neurofeedback process. Dr. Sunita Punjabi, also known as the Brain Coach, assists my family and me during neurofeedback.

After completing an assessment that addresses social dysfunction, anxiety, depression, loss of confidence, and depression scale, it will generate a report that will serve as the foundation for understanding what is going on with my brain zones and begin the training session that will assist me in correcting detected imbalances. I won't get into specifics because some topics are beyond my expertise, and I don't want to mislead you, but my experience has been excellent.

The good news is that you can go through this process with others. You can get started by reading books, listening to the audio, or watching videos that will take you to a particular stage of knowledge. However, you can shorten the learning curve and receive immediate results by contacting an expert and participating in a neurofeedback program.

This exercise is becoming increasingly popular since, in our competitive society, we require a sharper mind to act and react to various situations. During my quest, I became interested in Jim Kwik's work. I purchased his book "Limitless," which showed me that I could improve my brain, learn anything quickly, and unlock my extraordinary existence.

We overlook many things in our lives because we are so fixated on that dazzling object or novelty that our attention is drawn away. Our attention spans are quite short since we live in a crowded environment; therefore, we must clean our minds and limit stimulation.

One example is my strained relationship with my father; we have a formal Father-Son relationship. However, as you get older and become a parent, you attempt to avoid the mistakes you made as a child in order to provide your best and break the link for that recurrent cycle.

After learning this concept, it took me less than a month to reconcile with my father and shift our vibe. It also helped me cope with my mother's death more quickly. It's astonishing how this simple activity of recalling and upgrading memories has changed my life.

It took me more than 44 years to mend my relationship with my father and around 5 months to accept my mother's death. I'm grateful now and have a terrific relationship with my father. My memories of my mother have changed and grown into something quite new. I feel her presence every day, even if she is not physically present.
If you truly desire change, I can assure you will find it. If you are unsure, ask or conduct a Google search. The variety of resources and expertise available will astound you. As previously said, the most crucial part is "Deciding to Act."

The Kung Fu Panda wisdom

This is an excerpt from the movie; hopefully, I will not ruin it for you. I'll highlight some quotes that really stick out. One feature of this animated film that I like is how things work for the main character compared to our present way of viewing chances provided only for us. We believe we are unworthy of this and that. That is the only way, and there is no other way.

I hope you are not prejudiced against the film because it is animated. The story falls short of your expectations for a movie about ordinary people. Throughout a series of events, the main guy accepts his fate. They use words like prophecy and destiny, written in the universe for you to fulfill; you cannot escape it. You can refer to God, The Universe, or whichever superior force you believe in in this circumstance.

We are here for a reason, and there are no coincidences in life. There is a grand master plan, and our portion is a role only we can perform. Our minds get so preoccupied with everything we give them, whether voluntarily or involuntarily, that it becomes difficult to see. But suppose we try our hardest, take our time, let things settle, and decrease the number of stimuli. In that situation, we will find solutions swiftly, implying that our life objectives and ambitions will become a reality sooner rather than later.

"Anything is possible when you have inner peace."
— Kung Fu Panda

Another thing to consider is our need for validation or proof that we are worthwhile. Everyone around us believes we have what it takes. We usually presume that we must carry something over our shoulders as a burden because we feel the weight and pressure. We're too obsessed with what it was and what it will be.

Many of us want to be in charge of our lives because our parents laid out a plan for us when we were little. But now that we're grownups and that strategy isn't working for us, we're frustrated or sad. We can direct our fate and make decisions whenever we feel ready. Many of us have been in life-altering situations. Not because it's stated on our calendar on X Day of X Year. You will start your business, begin your career studies, start a new family, establish that successful partnership, and many other things.

Assume you believe that such things have never happened to you. In that scenario, you should watch the movie and pay close attention when the main character is doubting himself and trying to figure out what is happening. Until the "solution" was disclosed.
Sometimes the response is unexpected. This is an excellent opportunity to clarify the distinction

between mentality and mindfulness. Because the answer will drive you to question your views and allow your thoughts to develop acceptance or rejection, accepting that a new trait can be gained unfathomable for the entrenched attitude; nonetheless, if you have a growth attitude, you will embrace them because it can be developed and strengthened.

However, if you know this, you have accepted the forced change, adapted, adjusted, and continued because most life situations compel us to act. And it is vital to determine what we take with us because we sometimes carry a lot of unnecessary weight. However, they are making progress and bringing about change. You must discard old or unwanted beliefs to embrace those new beliefs.

"There is a saying: Yesterday is history, tomorrow is a mystery, but today is a gift.
That is why it is called the present."
— Kung Fu Panda

That is a wonderful bit of advice right there. Maybe you don't like the movie background, but if you live long enough, you will discover that God or the Universe will send messages through many channels.

The question that emerges here is:

Are you taking notes?

It will only be perceived as an opportunity if you have a fixed perspective. Your mindfulness will activate those negative ideas and opinions about yourself.

How would you react if you discovered a means to transform your fixed attitude into a growth mindset?

Will you accept the challenge and be willing to embrace and accept it?

If you do, here are five strategies for shifting from a fixed attitude to a growth mindset:

Cut the blame: Have you ever played a video game or a sporting event? If not, you put in more effort and continue to play when you lose. Keep things in perspective and avoid overreacting because no one gets it right the first time.

Do not run comparations: It is okay to be yourself; you are unique and comparing yourself to others serves no purpose other than to feed your stuck mentality. It's acceptable to be yourself.

Build Self-Awareness: This method will force you to consider if you are striving hard enough and whether your strategy is sound. It is critical to accomplish your growth mindset in this manner because you will be confronted with your old and new behaviors.

If you need clarification on this step, refer back to stages one and two.

Review and Assess: Remember when we discussed planning? You want to change, and your goals will guide you in that direction. If something isn't operating correctly, you should put forth the extra effort.

Remember, you don't have to waste time criticizing yourself or others. If something isn't working properly, let's fix it and move on. Blaming and complaining will not get you anywhere.

Celebrate small victories: Celebrating every accomplishment is the most effective method to transform your entrenched perspective. For example, you have already achieved multiple triumphs by performing your daily routine before beginning your commute to work. Your home and personal To-Do list items are completed. You're already on your way to work with two victories under your belt.

Please believe in yourself and your ability to change and improve; various resources can assist you in this endeavor. Listening is one of the most humbling components of asking for aid and comments.

If you ask for guidance but cannot attempt or listen, you will never be able to shift your entrenched perspective; this is a life hack you still need to include.

Chapter 3

"If life were predictable, it would cease
to be life and be without flavor."
-Eleanor Roosevelt

Pursuing your freedom

We will maintain the various meanings of the word freedom. We will stick to two premises in the context of this book: One is discovering what is holding you back from pursuing your destined glory. The second is about creating strategies to transform your beliefs and habits in seeking happiness.

I emphasize this because these two themes are so vast that we must go into the law. About your freedom in society, and so many other topics that will divert our attention away from the main purpose of this book. Thank you very much for being so patient!

One of the key conceptions we have for freedom is the will to be whatever we choose, and to help you explain, "capacity" is used instead of "will." Because you may have the will, but you think it will tell you otherwise, and you will end up back where you started.

The title of this book is "The Invisible Chain," as you can see. We refer to being free, independent, and without constraints, because you have discovered that you previously had a fixed attitude about your ability to learn a new skill that would help you advance in your career, current work, or even in your career organization.

My primary goal in creating my first book was to assist folks like you and me in breaking free from the rat race and establishing a prosperous lifestyle. As a result, individuals may have a better life, feeling satisfied and valued for their contributions to the organizations that employ them. Then I discovered a rat race for wealthy individuals because they hoard their money and are unable to spend it.

I was reading a book by Bob Proctor a few months back. He mentioned a neighbor he had when he was younger who lived like a pauper, and when he died, the cops discovered more than $100,000 in cash all around his house. That is a terrible story, and what is more disturbing is that people like Bob Proctor's boyhood neighbor exist in the present. Perhaps even closer than you realize because many of us have a strained relationship with the money and freedom that follow us.

When you comprehend and actively embrace freedom, you will manage your time and focus on your desires. I also provide time management coaching, and one of the most important components of learning how to manage your time is that you gain the freedom to run your day however you choose. Sometimes we complicate ourselves so much that we begin to carry other people's troubles and allow them to take up residence in our life.

"The 4-Hour Workweek" by Timothy Ferris is the book I'm currently reading. You must adopt new concepts and automate income rather than rely on classic wealth methods because you do not have to postpone your life till retirement. Their principles are correct if you ask. You must recognize that you will have to put in a lot of effort to create the income streams that would allow you to generate money automatically. Then, select a company or trusted individuals to handle the process for you. My first book discusses starting a side hustle, selling your knowledge and abilities, and making money. It is possible to have an automatic or passive income in our current life span. We must act now before it is too late.

If you want to be free. And by that, I mean:

- I want the freedom to… spend time with my family
- I want the freedom to… be or express myself
- I want the freedom to… find inner peace
- I want the freedom to… do what I love
- I want the freedom to… fulfill my dreams

The list might go on forever. It is a goal you seek; remember that the purpose of this book is to assist you in determining what is preventing you from achieving your destined grandeur.

Creating a strategy for your growth

Many of us are perplexed when it comes to growing methods since it is not what we were sold. Most of us can't answer that question because we associate growth with things we already know. For example, professional development entails continuing to study until you obtain your Ph.D. If only one, more than a second Ph.D. is required.

What we're talking about here is that your growth strategy includes personal development, which is ultimately a self-improvement process. Under normal circumstances, we have a tendency to react to whatever comes into our lives. Because we interact with different scenarios on a regular basis, that process becomes more accessible as we grow.

Follow these six stages to help you write your growth strategies:

Step one: One of the most important measures we need to take to begin our growth process is to assess where we are now. What is your life like right now, and how will it be in the future? Making that initial assessment will give you a powerful perspective on your life. You have a place to begin for the things you are not proud of or need to better.

To comprehend what you lack, you must first grasp what you have. Create a chronology, a collection of activities or experiences, and begin with tiny steps.

Step two: You must examine your health because everything is interconnected. How you eat, sleep, whom you hang out with, and many other aspects all contribute to your overall health. Today, we have a plethora of vitamins and supplements at our disposal that can assist us in correcting our digestive imbalance. Furthermore, we are creatures designed for movement. Thus, you must exercise.

Everything works in unison, and if you ate well the night before, you're likely to enjoy a good night's sleep. As a result, you wake up before your alarm the next day because your body is well-rested and energized to work out or meditate.

If you want to progress, taking care of your temple will put you on the right track.

Remember that we are whole and must balance our efforts in all areas.

Step three: Make a strategy and define goals. Steps one and two have shown you what you have and don't have. The next step is to create your plan, which includes a list of actions needed to attain your new vision.

Assume you require assistance in making strategies and setting goals. In that case, please get in touch with us so we can assist you in creating a killer strategy, breaking it down into milestones, and generating tasks that can be broken into subtasks. It doesn't sound very easy, but it's a lot of fun.

Step four: Never stop learning. Because every time you have the chance to improve in a subject, the more you understand that you have very little information and that there is a vast ocean of knowledge to assimilate, process, and apply, the humbler you become as you continue to study.

Step five: Control your time. I apologize if I seem like a broken record. The fact is that time is a precious resource that cannot be recovered. Distractions and algorithms are actively attempting to grab our attention. And as we saw in step three, you must have a strategy to avoid distractions because trash content is everywhere.

I'm not suggesting you cancel your Netflix subscription or relocate to a remote region. You need a time management approach. Having a plan and a method to deal with time-wasting activities is simple because you can watch a Netflix marathon of your favorite series without feeling guilty. The goal is that after the show, you should find something to do with your time instead of browsing about and watching things that are uninteresting to you and will distract you.
It would be ideal if you had a timer as well. Yes, that little irritant. The reason you need one of those is to give you an idea of how much time has gone. In my instance, I utilize a single program that runs a countdown counter for 25 minutes, which greatly aids my concentration. And because I can see the end of time approaching, my sense of completeness kicks in, and my time is more effective.

I've been utilizing the Pomodoro technique for over a decade. A To-Do list and those simple but effective tools enabled me to develop ideas, projects, and possibilities that I would never have considered before.

Step Six: Create a circle of like-minded people. This is one of the most accessible venues for humbly testing your knowledge. When you meet others who share your interests, your knowledge will grow since they will discuss topics that you are interested in. Social media platforms are an excellent way to communicate with people worldwide. You will be exposed to many points of view, which will be an enriching experience.

You can add more steps; the most essential thing is that you have them close at hand and primarily complete them every day until your goals are accomplished and a new set of goals is required.

Creating a personal strategy

Most of us are working on developing a personal strategy that will be followed by the question: Why?

You can list things you want to change in your life; perhaps your energy is focused on finding a better career that will provide you prestige and recognition. Pursue the degree to help you gain the knowledge you need to enter the field you want to work in. Create that extra source of income you need to get out of the rat race, or simply take the plunge to become an entrepreneur and fulfill many more goals.

Choose a goal and allow me to share one of my experiences with you.

I used to be quite picky about what I read a few years ago. Because I was only interested in technical content, and when possibilities arose to study other types of books on diverse topics, my initial reaction was rejection. Even my verbal response was that I was not interested in that type of material. I am fascinated by computers and everything somewhat related to them.

And, of course, because I work in a competitive and ever-changing environment. Everyone must be aware of the most recent trends, rumors, and industry projections. As a result, I limited the number of people who could understand and discuss it. I couldn't hold a conversation with my family members or colleagues since the issue was so deep and sophisticated that they would need a lot of time to understand what I was saying.

Honestly, I had no reason to refuse other types of content since I felt I needed to be on top of my game. Other aspects of my life, though, required my attention. My family also wanted to know how I could be constant and disciplined.

Then I began to explain the approaches and techniques I employed back then. When I told my wife Diana how I was doing, she told me, "You need to share this with everyone because you can help a lot of people." From there, I launched my time management and business launch coaching programs and consulting services.

My day is dynamic; that is where most people get confused about time management. The main reason for this is that people identify time management with the task you used to get paid for, which means you must clock in when you start working and clock out when you leave for lunch. Clock back in after lunch and out when you leave work to go home.

That is not time management, believe me.

I set aside time for work because I work on a project with my full attention. When the timer goes off, I go on to the next activity since my priority is to be as efficient as possible in the allotted minutes.

This highlights the significance of developing a strategy and putting it into action. If you work on your daily tasks and goals for a year, you will have 365 days for 25-minute blocks of time. Assume you decide to work on your project by developing a plan. You define your goals, break them down into milestones, and perform tasks and subtasks. You will have 9,125 minutes in one year, equal to 6.34 full days.

And to be honest, if you devote that much time to your pursuits, your life will alter forever. Because once you begin to notice change and growth, you will like the process, and these work blocks will become a habit, bypassing the 21 or 22-day milestone. They will be a part of your life in three months.

I was fascinated by the idea of uploading and downloading information from our brains as we do with computers or mobile devices. Consider the potential of an app that enables us to learn a new skill. Installing a software update to update our beliefs and obtain the most recent version will be fantastic. We'd be wonderful in no time, overcoming our concerns by downloading an app or updating. For those who enjoy hacking and cracking systems, this will be a playground of possibilities to explore how far you can go in extending and changing your thoughts.

Remember. There is no shortcut to this; you can easily overcome anything you choose.

Tools & Tips to Manage Your Time and Defeat Procrastination

Let us begin with logic; many people allude to, discuss, and have formed an image of procrastination. What we'll do is learn the facts. The meaning and how it affects us are two facts.

Procrastination
Noun
the act or habit of procrastinating, or putting off or delaying, especially something requiring immediate attention: She was smart, but her constant procrastination led her to be late with almost every assignment.

Word origin and history of procrastination
n.

The 1540s, from Middle French procrastination and directly from Latin procrastinationem (nominative procrastinatio), "a putting off from day to day," noun of action from past participle stem of procrastinare "put off till tomorrow, defer, delay," from pro- "forward" (see pro-) + crastinus "belonging to tomorrow," from cras "tomorrow," of unknown origin.

That is the definition found on dictionary.com; here is the link https://www.dictionary.com/browse/procrastinatio n.

We understand, based on the definition of procrastination, which is a healthy or unhealthy habit. Let's get started. I know that many people operate better under pressure. However, in order to achieve that level, you must learn to manage your time and arrange your workload; otherwise, you will be overwhelmed with anxiety. That is something you should work on. Our first conclusion was that we have many negative habits. You haven't noticed it yet because they haven't affected you, but you require a review. However, for those habits that are causing you problems, there is an urgent need to devise a strategy to overcome those habits.

All this is very important, and you need to write this down and put it in a visible place everywhere you are, in your workspace, in your house, car, mobile, etc. *"You can't get rid of a bad habit; instead, you change it."*

Repeat after me: *"You can't get rid of a bad habit; instead, you change it."*

Being on time somewhere is a tough challenge for many people. This affects both children and adults, and the causes are simple. One example is not sleeping and eating properly, distractions, and a lack of structure. Numerous factors can provide a challenge to us as we want to be better or to be the next version. If we want to change or discover a way to pursue our interests, we must take the first step. Otherwise, we won't be able to modify ourselves and will remain trapped.

As you can see, this is another link in your "invisible chain," a stumbling block. We don't know what it is, and the solution is, "we need to change our behaviors and even early beliefs that were ingrained in us as children." Changing our reality perspective with an open mind can allow us to attain our goals and solve numerous pre-programmed problems in ourselves. You will need to make a few changes in your life beginning today. Remember this book's major goal: to provide insights into what is going on with yourself. And discover the true reason "why you can't change your life" so that you can pursue your dreams and live happily ever after.

I am a firm believer in self-control and motivation. Good habits inspire you; whatever your intentions are, you will achieve them, and with self-control, you will have the set of rules necessary to fulfill your goals. Even if you are sad or depressed, you will have a behavior modification plan in place to keep things from spiraling out of control. To effectively deal with procrastination and achieve your goals. We will work on a "Project Management structure," which requires you to divide the project into tiny, attainable milestones and define completion time frames and due dates.

Creating everyday work habits comes in extremely handy here. You can utilize a variety of tools (digital or on paper) to assist you in becoming a go-getter.

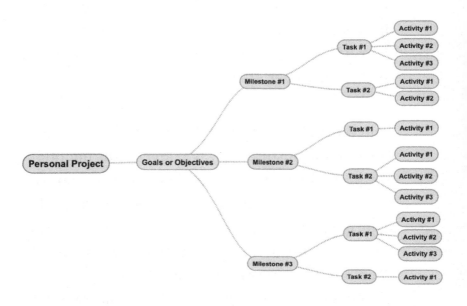

Remember, the goal is to establish healthy routines. We are not automating monotonous jobs or filling your day so completely that you can barely eat. Most of us have probably heard of "the schedule" at school or work, where we were assigned 45 to 55 minutes to work on a specific subject or activity (Productivity habit). They assigned us homework, and if we didn't complete it or turn it in on time, we would face the repercussions.

This feature will provoke a reaction from us: fear, anxiety, a sense of accomplishment, joy, and you name it. Many people call this a discipline. It also fosters abstinence in all areas relating to word discipline. It's merely a conditional command that gets stuck in our thoughts all the time:

Discipline = Success

Vs.

Indiscipline = Failure

As a result, from now on, we will speak to "SELF-CONTROL" rather than "DISCIPLINE." You have a "mental recall" from the past associated with "a physical reaction and emotion" when you hear that term. I've asked numerous friends, and they all feel goosebumps when they hear the term "discipline." They recall something from their middle or high school years. Memories of a specific class, for example, the Professor always spoke in a deep tone or yelled. The mix of using your entire name and last name drew your attention. There was an awkward silence in the classroom, and everyone was staring at you.

From then on, you feel chills whenever you hear phrases like that. Perhaps when your full name addresses you as an adult, you might ask yourself, "Oh, am I in any trouble?"

It is best to learn how to deal with oneself when words cause dread in you and you are willing to adjust the energy at the time or, better yet, grasp how to let it go. Working with "self-control" will allow you to restart this new process, replace old habits, and develop new ones in this new part of your inner change trip.

A good habit provides us with a sense of self-realization, and today we must go into our inner selves to recall those days in school when we were given a homework assignment with a deadline. Because it was a priority, you worked hard and spent a respectable amount of time on it. Remember those occasions; you can redirect your energy to seek your long-term reward, the next version of yourself. The doer and the go-getter!

It will be important to be able to replace negative habits and adjust your behavior. You now know what to do when the old bad habit returns. That will be the key to your success in replacing your undesirable habits.

Change is obstinate; determination, self-control, and consistency are intended to make your goal a reality. You should read the entire book if you agree with the previous statement. Making excuses and feeling sorry for yourself is not a recipe for success. Change your bad behaviors to become a better version of yourself. Most of us nowadays are desperate for a way to pursue our dreams in life. We will need something tangible to reach and feel to keep moving forward, such as tips, formulas, or methods.

Most importantly, be modest and recognize that you require assistance; we are all human beings. This chaotic world bombards us with distractions and temptations on a daily basis. I'm confident you'll come up with a solution shortly. All you have to do is identify and plan a strategy to follow and pursue your passions in life. Keep in mind that this will not be a simple or quick path. It will take all of your efforts to achieve success.

So, in order to achieve our life goals, we must have a mechanism in place to maintain Self-Control. Many people make light of the fact that many are engrossed in books and do not enjoy life.

Successful entrepreneurs, on the other hand, read a variety of books on mentality, self-improvement, and other topics. Our nature is flawed. We must accept it and learn to live with it. For many people, perfection is a state that is temporary and not permanent. It's a gift, and we should learn to appreciate it while we can.

Here's an example. I don't know how many of you own or have owned a dog. After bathing, thoroughly cleaning, and even brushing it, you let it loose, and your dog runs around your house, towards your yard, and rolls in your grass. It makes no difference how hard you try to clean your dog. You had a brief moment of perfection when your dog was groomed and looked spotless until it arrived in your yard.

According to studies, it can help you master "Self-Control," and some suggest that "if you perform an action for 22 days, it will become a habit." Another method, dubbed "21/90," asserts that it takes 21 days to form a habit and 90 days to establish a lifestyle. I made a tangible notebook journal. You can obtain and track your habit modification process by visiting https://eliacevedo.com.

If you want to change your approach, you must first provide the first step. And it all starts with determination and dedication. Organizing your time and daily schedule, finishing your to-do list on a daily basis, and trying hard to stick to your plan no matter what comes up. Completing each milestone and not losing sight of your work and other activities in your life. There are numerous interruptions and attention grabbers, and it is easy to become engulfed in the distraction wave.

If you require assistance in this area, seek a time management program, a coach, or a mentor, and be willing to accept all ideas and advice offered. Keep learning those procedures and activities; you can do it. You've tried it before, and it didn't work as intended. The experience I obtained over my coaching journey enabled me to discover numerous things. A rigorous plan with a start and end date is the best approach for a person to learn something and apply it to his life.

Over the years, I have had to alter and set an expiration date for my coaching programs. And once you've begun the program, you must complete each phase in order to complete it. I used to let individuals do it at their own pace, the "Self-Paced Method," but very few people completed the entire program; they constantly pushed it off and made excuses.

After I modified the system of my program, most of my students completed it and were delighted with it; that change is the most effective way to have a tiny boss saying you, do this, do that. Until you acquire self-control, rely on the method, and implement it into your life.

Assume you want to do it right now but need the money. If you like, you could apply for a loan, sell some old antiques in your home, cupcakes and lemonade, or anything else that comes to mind; don't be afraid to invest in yourself. You are currently taking a financial risk in order to enhance your life. Don't be terrified if this is your first time; this is the first step toward regaining control of your life and breaking free from that invisible chain.

You will only find a fit between your finances and aspirations if you have control. Take the risk. If you don't feel like it, you could read my other book,

"Being Broke No More," which will provide you with essential insights to help you get started on the path to prosperity. If you wish to have a look, here is the link: https://eliacevedo.com/books/being-broke-no-more/

After finishing Being Broke No More, I began writing this book because many aspects of the attitude needed to be explained and, for the most part, worked. It's not just saying the words while people are looking at you; it's also how you act when you're alone, in your office, at home, and so on. When you begin this new challenge and make this new commitment, everything in your life will improve, including your financial health. I'm not claiming it will be simple; you may have setbacks as part of the learning process. We learn from our errors.

Be present. It's your life, and you have power over it. If you feel someone owns you, it's time to take action and get help. Look for a program online if you feel lonely and the people around you cannot assist you. If you are still looking for someone who meets your requirements, visit https://eliacevedo.com and make time from your current schedule.

Being a free person necessitates organization. You could do it yourself or pay someone to manage your schedule. You must also maintain your wealth and investments and seek proper assistance. They are daily work tasks that cannot be overlooked and delegated as much as possible. You would not completely withdraw from your firm, and some problems will require your time and attention at some point. Besides, there's no reason to remain away if you enjoy what you're doing. Controlling your life necessitates organization and self-control. You don't want individuals wasting your time or making you late for an appointment, do you?

As I previously stated, you must learn how to become an organized person with your agenda. If you are not capable, hire someone to do it for you.

I've collaborated with a number of people over the years. Some of them are unable to put it together, not because they do not wish to. It's something unexplainable that prevents them from progressing. You could even call it self-sabotage. Then I had a hardship when one of my sons was affected by a problem. I utilized all of my motivational arsenals with no success, which was disappointing. That made me know it was something other than self-control and motivation. To design an action plan, I needed to delve deeper into the reason.

All of this prompted me to look for new solutions to determine why individuals couldn't adjust in good or bad weather. We all know that there is no secret pill, quick fix, shortcut, book, or podcast to locate the cause; it is a process of self-discovery. It would be preferable if you worked on your discoveries during your voyage.

It will be difficult, and we will make mistakes, as with anything we do for the first time, but it will be honest and clear. You will eventually understand when it is time, figure out how to do it, and recognize when the change has occurred. It's what I call "the awakening." People today blame social media, the economy, the government, and online video platforms. They want to be held accountable for having many people interested and involved in their series and distracted from their goals, yet all they are doing is transferring guilt.

I use an online platform and social media; the actual secret is to "know when to stop"; no platform can tell you what to do next. This is where having a "To-Do List" handy comes in helpful. You will have pending duties that you cannot ignore. That will influence you to adjust your conduct; you might leap two or three times instead of staying connected the entire time and letting the term "Marathon" sink in. You will have to continue doing all your daily activities while exercising mental reasoning. You'll be able to control it as quickly as I can.

A few days ago, I saw an interesting and manipulative ad from Netflix on my "Facebook feed" about a show. The text stated: "Don't be left out of the conversation." That is a forced behavior ad and almost a social threat. Perhaps a command said, "If you don't want people excluding you in the conversation," "you must watch the show," and you will be socially accepted. You can be part of the "X Series" or "Show title." I think it isn't very nice. If you feel pressure, remember to put yourself first, get your cheat sheet for good/bad behaviors, and stick to your list to avoid distraction. Focusing on your goals and happiness while watching a show or a series to give you conversation material is far from your dreams. Fiction stories are just fantasy stories.

In my case, I have a designated time in my day to entertain myself. I have the same quantity of hours you have. I use social platforms and online streaming services. Sometimes my work requires pushing off my free or entertainment time. I move dynamically to my schedule, which means the most important things get done first in chunks of time. If I have a problem or get stuck, I move to the next item on my to-do list; later, I'll revisit the problematic/unsolved task and move on.

I've got plenty of time to catch up on my other commitments. It all comes down to committing to and prioritizing what is vital and must be completed. Don't get me wrong: I'm working and doing something I enjoy. The border between joy and work is quite thin. All of this makes me proud of what I've created with my wife; it's simply a matter of catching up and being serious about DOING what it takes to reach your goals.

Assume you struggle to manage your time at work or home while running your home-based business with your assigned chores. Productivity Programs are available in that instance, but you require a Time Management Program.

What is the distinction, you may wonder?

The short version is that a productivity program focuses on employees accomplishing a lot of work while limiting coworker chat, coffee, and toilet time. It was primarily concerned with monitoring every minute of your work time or shift. It also shifts production obligations to workers, requiring them to arrive physically and emotionally prepared to work their butts off.

A time management program varies in that it separates work and personal interests, allowing for mental relaxation. People can't focus solely on work and ignore a sick relative, personal finances, or even their health. Everything should be in harmony, and once the program is in place, you will be more efficient in working less time. Old and harmful behaviors will be broken. You don't have to "appear busy" in your business or home.

Assume you or your team need help managing your work time precisely. In such case, I have established another software specifically for businesses for you. Obtain the assistance you or your team require to optimize your workflow or schedule. Most crucial, complete all your responsibilities so that you may focus on your dreams or goals in life. Controlling your time is the true secret to living an extraordinary life. Be present for anything you care about! Your professional activities, workouts, business, projects, trips, family, you name it, and attaining your life goals.

As I previously stated, it molded us with structured behaviors in our early years, and there is a better method to do it (in terms to change, obviously). However, we should hack into it and make it work for us in order to achieve our aspirations and goals. At the moment, we need to find another word to replace "Schedule"; let's try replacing it with "Agenda" and create a plan for each of our goals. You are now learning how to cultivate your new superpower, a combination of "Self-Control" and "Agenda," for this new version of yourself, your 2.0 version.

I'm an early riser. I like completing all my hobbies, such as working out, meditating, and reading, before breakfast. And spend time with my family before diving into my projects, businesses, or planned activities. I value punctuality, don't mind waiting, and plan and calculate routes to account for probable delays.

However, imagine you devote more time than you should to one hobby. Your list will be impacted in that instance, causing other tasks to fall behind or go unfinished. You must prioritize and set a time limit and maintain control over your agenda. Please make sure your timetable covers the whole day; you must leave room for unforeseen events and be able to move your short and extended breaks.

Please do not become "the Doctor No," not having time for other things because they are not on your list, because you have control and can make the necessary modifications to move place quickly. At this point, you must commit yourself to overcoming obstacles to a better life, work, self-growth, and wonderful health. Finding your weakness is the first reconnaissance task, leading you to confront your temptations and good/bad behaviors.

Now is the moment to write it big and devise an attacking strategy. You must prepare to battle negative habits and praise positive ones and work on them continuously until you win control. You will gain self-control by devising a strategy you must be aware of. Remember, you're in control and on the right track; I'm confident you can do it.

If you have a skin infection, the process is similar; you cannot heal it immediately. First, you must eliminate the illness (if any). Then apply lotions and take care of your skin until it totally recovers; keep it clean and fresh, and repeat as needed. You know you can't rush it, and if you ignore your treatment, it may become infected (if it wasn't already) and require further treatment and attention. And if you don't treat it properly once it has healed, you will have an unsightly scar as a result of how you were handled.

This is the initial plan. You will now do the same with your weak spot, working on it little by little until you get mastery of your thoughts. Be prepared if this unhealthy habit, behavior, or incorrect thought triggers.

You only have a few seconds to change it (five or fewer seconds); therefore, it is critical to know what will happen following the action on your list. You are now aware of what will happen next, leaving no room for speculation. Check your agenda beforehand; this will help you stay focused.

Controlling your negative thoughts by writing them down will help to lessen everyday desires and send a mindful response. The replacement will be helpful to have on hand. An excellent habit substitute will change how you feel or think. If you don't have it, a hunger reward will set in and cause you to succumb to temptation.

You must be aware that you will be the only one who can do this for yourself and no one else. That will be a contract between you and your inner self to improve yourself through healthy habits and be free to pursue your dreams. Let's move on and figure out what's causing all of this, shall we?

Chapter 4

"Your time is limited, so don't waste it living someone else's life. Don't be trapped by dogma — which is living with the results of other people's thinking."
-Steve Jobs

Planning your Work

You've undoubtedly heard this a few times, and I'm afraid I'm getting on your nerves. However, my experience has shown me that planning is essential. It's not that I'm OCD about preparing everything; it's simply that the parts you want to change that you've determined need better, and if money is one of them, work on them. If you have money and are miserable, there you have it.

You can make planning as simple or as complicated as you want, but we're attempting to be objective and operate with logic. We will only focus on preparing for your job, but once you learn and gain it, you will utilize it in your personal life and aspirations.

You must follow a few steps; some can be completed sooner. For example, you cannot close and ship a box unless it contains content. You can advance by assembling many boxes based on the number of orders received, no more, no less, just the proper quantity.

Every piece of work necessitates a path of achievement in order to attain a goal; this is referred to as a start and endpoint procedure. There are a few rest breaks along the way. First, when it is born, you have established your first process, which is working, but you will eventually examine it and seek improvements. The argument will always be cost and productivity; optimizing a process will save you time and money.

When you examine a process closely, you will consider leveraging resources (workforce, space, technology, etc.). Each company has a restricted capacity due to people, space, storage, or other issues. A restaurant is a good example. It can only seat a limited number of people and currently serves only a few clients. Several operations are involved, including receiving orders, preparing meals, cooking, and assisting at the table.

That is an example of teamwork. You can even discover a live model at your next restaurant meal.

Take a break and consider the following:

How many servers are there?
How long does it take to receive your order?

The most significant time to monitor this is during peak hours; it's the best time to examine resource utilization, and the result will be your meal experience.

The wait time was appropriate for the food you requested.
Did the table service meet or exceed your expectations?
Had the cuisine fulfilled your expectations?
You may now judge how well that restaurant performs overall. We will not strive for perfection, which is an idea for a faultless state. We shall concentrate on achieving our objectives.

Remember, we will concentrate our efforts on your work, the work you are doing; we have a few essential actions you must do to achieve your objectives, working smart rather than hard.

- Setting goals.
- Prioritize your tasks.
- Plan ahead.

- Learn to say no.
- Avoid distractions.
- Delegate.
- Maximize your time.
- Breathe and meditate.

Setting goals

That isn't rocket science and has something to do with time management. It intends to keep you focused on actions to help you achieve your business goals.

Keeping yourself in the game allows you to provide your clients with what they expect. Doing the right thing will help your business obtain the momentum it needs to take off. It will bring your dreams of money, growth, and recognition to fruition.

SMART goals are a way to help firms focus on tasks and deadlines (Specific, Measurable, Attainable, Relevant, and Time-bound). The syntax is straightforward; you establish a clear goal and go step by step.

Once you've learned how to implement it into your work, it will be simple because you'll know who can manage each assignment. You are now free of the strain of doing everything yourself while waiting for someone to come and offer your assistance.

This strategy will help you and your business run more smoothly. Be more productive, and most importantly, set you on the right track to attaining your objectives.

Prioritize your tasks

This is one of the trickiest sections that can impede achieving your objectives; we must complete all tasks. However, learning how to classify what should go first would be beneficial. You may discover and test it by making a list and categorizing it according to priority, as shown below:

High priority – What is crucial and urgent: You are aware that this must be completed as quickly as possible.

Priority – What is critical but not urgent: They are necessary and can be addressed once high-priority tasks have been completed.

Mid priority – What is urgent but not important: You can schedule a time during the day to work on these chores, have deadlines, and know when priority tasks are completed or whether they require the assistance of a third party.

Low priority – What is not urgent or important: Do not be misled by low-priority chores. They are an essential component of the objective. You can make plans, but you must carry them out. You don't want a low-priority task to become a high-priority just because it wasn't completed on time.

Each task will have an order of execution by splitting any goal down with a priority label. Your company will have a sense of accomplishment, boosting motivation and productivity.

Plan ahead.

You must learn that for yourself and then share that with the rest of your company. This is also a part of my Time Management Program. It's great to write down anything on your mind about work and put it on your to-do list. Then it's over immediately before your workday or shifts; you know what you need to do the next morning. Your thinking will be calmer, and you will enjoy and rest well.

You'll know exactly what you need to work on the next day. You may also use your to-do list to analyze your workday and assign priority. You keep track of where tasks are completed and stick to your goals and deadline, inspiring others to perform at their best.

Learn to say no

Changing the management team's mind may be difficult if you are an employee. Nonetheless, because it concentrates on the higher goal's tasks, it will help you learn how to say no to other team members.
But imagine you're the owner or president. In that situation, it will bombard you with activities and invitations that will keep you from achieving your objectives. You can give up some of your time and work extremely early in the morning. Make time for these events in order to expand your commercial network with other business owners and possible clients.

All other activities are classified as timewasters and should be avoided simply by saying no.

Avoid distractions.

Distractions are many entrepreneurs' and creative minds' kryptonite; they also impact productivity because they make it difficult to focus quickly. That is something you must cultivate and learn from your team. It would be best if you also liberated yourself.

Distractions can be managed by understanding how to rely on your team. If they have to ask you every 5 minutes along the route, it shows you need to communicate more effectively or are unwilling to distribute duties.

We'll get to that later. However, if clients cause distractions, you cannot escape them. You must set aside time when you may work entirely concentrated with no interruptions. After that, notify everyone that you are available; as always, you must be prepared if there is an emergency. You can use approaches like the Pomodoro Technique. If you have trouble concentrating, they are simple to use; you may set timers of 25, 30, or 35 minutes to work on a task and progress. We can't remove or prevent distractions; we need a strategy to cope with them, complete tasks, and increase productivity.

Delegate

That is a huge difficulty for most people because the first issue with delegation is having a negative expectation of the outcome. You may have high hopes or even wish for them to fail. You're making a point or crossing a boundary by claiming that you're unique and that things can't be done at the same level but for you.

As you read this section, you will most likely express your concern about being replaced or not giving your all to your firm, among other things. You must organize your thoughts and remember why you hired your existing staff. They are there to help you run your business; none of them will legally take control of it. They will, however, be there for you if you create a healthy work atmosphere, and you must trust them.

When you employ someone to join your team, you ask them what they can do for your company based on your requirements. And ultimately, you should let them do what they have indicated they can do for your company. If they can't back up their commitments, I'm sure they'll depart your organization. You are not required to let them go.

The whole idea of hiring new employees is to increase productivity. As the owner or leader, you have the ability to free up time; learning to delegate will be crucial. Instead of doing them yourself, you might delegate and manage time-consuming tasks.
If you are afraid of delegating, we can assist you in overcoming your phobia. And you can fix that by developing an online course, program, or procedure. It's a matter of desiring a solution. Consider having more time to think about new initiatives, construct proposals, or improve your business.

You can continually improve any employee or student. You only need to create the right environment and equipment to become a reality. If you believe they are talented, you can teach them the skills they need to improve or create a mentorship program to meet your requirements. You'll be in better shape and have more leisure time.

Maximize your time

Because time is a finite resource, it is one of our most pressing concerns in modern civilization. Every day, we can only give 23 hours and 59 minutes. We must be aware of how much time we waste when we lack control.

We understand schedules and timing. But we could be happier with learning the fundamentals of efficient time management. This occurs because we need to track our time. When it is close to lunchtime, we are usually anxious about our time, especially if we are hungry or weary and want to go home.

Many organizations utilize time trackers since keeping track of each team member while working, taking a break, or leaving for the day is challenging. Many employees follow a schedule in which they must work 40 hours per week and are paid overtime if they surpass that period. However, you should work 80 or more weekly hours if you are an entrepreneur or business owner. That is debatable. We will need to talk about what you do

80 hours a week if you are not manufacturing a product that requires someone to produce it.

You can improve this by tracking your time and managing your workday better. You may create a priority list, allot work time, and split large jobs into smaller ones. It will astound you how many minor tasks can be completed by breaking them down into bits and delegating what can be allocated.

You must be mindful of your time and prevent distractions in your everyday routine.
Remember that having a full day is not a good idea because you have yet to allow room for issues or circumstances. This is an excellent case for implementing the Pomodoro technique.

Breathe and meditate

You must rest; learn how to do it and include it into your daily routine; we are not robots. We become weary when we do not eat or sleep correctly. I don't need to cite studies to explain why this is crucial.

I used this strategy a few years ago when my mind and body were fatigued after a long day at work. I was under much stress, and because I wasn't taking care of my health at work, things weren't going as well as they should.

I've learned to work more efficiently by structuring my work time. It took a lot of time, but I could adjust my time with clients and tasks while still developing strategies and ideas to improve my business.

I need to learn a lot about rest and all of the benefits it may provide. The first is to take some deep breaths. It takes between two and five minutes to meditate with your eyes closed. You may fall asleep at first because you are fueling your body with oxygen or because you are tired. However, it would be best if you continued to try until you mastered it.

Here are five simple stages of meditation:

Make a whoosh sound as you exhale entirely through your mouth.
Close your mouth and take a five-count inhalation via your nose.
Hold your breath for five seconds.
Exhale entirely via your mouth to a count of ten, generating a whoosh sound.
That is only one breath. Make the most of your two or five minutes.

Every spin in the Pomodoro technique involves a five-minute rest. You get a fifteen-minute break every two or three revolutions. You can meditate for two or five minutes during this pause and then proceed to the next job on your to-do list. When your lunch break is approaching, plan for a 22-minute snooze.

This made me very skeptical. Because I don't drink coffee, I expected to be sluggish and sleepy all afternoon. My options for staying awake were limited. The first day of my journey was not pleasant. I slept for about 2 hours and was exhausted when I got home; it took me a while to fall asleep at my bedtime... not what I expected.

The next day, I achieved 21 minutes rather than the projected 22, but the thrill was incredible. I felt as if I had just awoken from a deep sleep. I felt energized, and all of my ideas flowed.
I was happy because I had completed numerous tasks that afternoon. My thoughts were not on work when I left my workplace. I put all job-related things on my to-do list, my work schedule was now orderly, and my mind was free when my workday was done.

That day, I felt an unexplainable sense of calm. Since then, I've understood that my work philosophy was incorrect, and the phrase "work smarter, not harder" has enlightened me.

My workday was never the same after that. I could increase my productivity, propelling my company forward with various new projects and clientele. I was living each day happier, the consequence of a few simple steps that completely improved my life, and this is the message I want to share with you.

I did it myself; I picked up some supplies and began with trial and error, and it worked. If you lack this determination, you might seek assistance with a time management program for workplace productivity as a starting point. This will improve your life, and having control over your time will help you overcome many of your concerns.

Productivity vs Effectiveness

You will appreciate each workday if you organize it and develop healthy routines. You will feel refreshed and joyful if you live stress-free and follow these simple measures to build good work habits:

Keep hydrated.

Understanding that drinking coffee is not the same as drinking water is critical. The number of people (both men and women) racing about your office who are adequately hydrated will astound you. There are typical symptoms of dehydration that your staff or you may experience without understanding the source.

Find sugar substitutes.

Sugars cause desires in our bodies. They also have little nutritional value. Your energy level will drop if you have a busy day filled with meetings, phone calls, and responding to emails. The more honest answer is to seek snacks to combat exhaustion, but you know yourself, so get some fruits and nuts instead of a large bag of Doritos or cheese balls. These will give you the necessary energy (vitamins and minerals) to carry you through the day.

Make use of active pauses.

Again, we are not machines and require regular movement. Standing up and stretching your legs, walking near a window to rest your eyes, sharing your shoulders, and moving your head are all necessary. Otherwise, you will lead a sedentary lifestyle that may harm your health.

Keep in mind the five- and fifteen-minute pauses. You can switch between meditation and active pauses. You can relieve the stress of being in the same posture for an extended period of time by reaching for the stairs and performing a quick workout.

As you wish to improve your circulation and posture at work, the alternatives are unlimited, which leads us to the following stage.

Your workplace postures.

We frequently disregard our stance. We still needed to learn how this impacts your mood and lowers lung function, resulting in less oxygenated blood to the brain. If you only use one monitor, you may experience neck aches.

You can get ergonomic chairs, such as a ball or kneeling chairs. You might spend a lot of money, but what matters is that you want to safeguard your body. The most valuable possession you have, the natural, is the ability to feel good. If you are in agony, you should seek medical attention right once. You are causing yourself harm and do not have enough money to ignore your symptoms.

Numerous gadgets and straps are available to assist you in maintaining good posture; however, consider them.

Create a pleasant working atmosphere.

The working environment may be different from what you imagined. It's easy to become caught up in the stress trap. However, by utilizing positive imagery, you can minimize the negative charge you are carrying. Including tranquil items can assist in transforming this tense environment into a quiet one.

The procedure is simple: clear your desk and place the order. Then incorporate positive affirmations, photos, or even a journal where you can remind yourself of your goals and why you are doing this. It can be insignificant enough for everyone to notice; you can do it in the corner of your workspace. Include an indoor plant, such as a flowering cactus, that stands out and provides joy when you need it the most.

Finish your day at the office.

Nowadays, having a home office or a computer to check work is common. It would be best if you stopped doing this. You need to give your brain a break from your daily obligations. You are feeding the worry of not providing your all at work and need to compensate. You don't need to steal your spare time to complete extra work if you've worked on your to-do list; everything is planned for the next day, milestones have deadlines, and the entire project is spelled out. If you haven't already, you should get started right away.

Remember that your brain does not rest; it recharges, and you must allow it to recharge adequately. You don't want to be mentally worn out. If anything urgent occurs, you can turn off your data after leaving your office; you are only a phone call away.

Spend your free time reading, going to the gym, walking your dog, riding your bike, visiting a park, enjoying nature, going out with a friend or spouse, playing with your kids, writing an e-book, and attending meetings. You can engage in a variety of practical activities. You are altering your entire way of life, and each day gives you the courage to overcome your anxieties and break the invisible chain you are wearing.

Managing your time to increase effectiveness, not productivity

Our primary goal is to improve effectiveness rather than productivity. Please keep this in mind.

This may appear contradictory because today's society expects everyone to be as productive as possible. Even we have allowed multitasking to take root in our life, attempting to perform multiple tasks with good quality in less time than intended. We can multitask in some situations but try writing a business proposal while attending a meeting. Please keep me updated on how things progress.

The secret is to concentrate. Things will flow smoothly, and you will be finished if you pay attention to what has to be done. It would be best if you learned how to concentrate when performing something. I'll guarantee you realize this at some point in time. You may have been putting something off for a long time and have finally decided to do it. You discovered that this was a pretty simple task.

You can do it because you have focused all your energy on this task or activity, but we will only get there if we learn to handle this talent "Focus.

" Consider our school days, when we were given limited time to listen to lectures on a particular subject.

That is because our brains can only handle a particular amount of information before becoming weary, and more things are in place when we are at work. As a result, time management approaches aid development rather than reminding you how many hours are left in the day, how much you earn per hour, or that you can only acquire a little time. It is all about focusing your attention on the task at hand.

Productivity is a means to an end that you can achieve by forcing yourself to unload a truck and create more things. One of the more difficult undertakings nowadays is writing a book because you need to be inspired to read, review, and edit what you've written.

After that, please send it to an editor to get your manuscript reviewed. Get their input and possibly revise any complex ideas. Then, reread the text, marking your editor's revisions, to ensure that your thoughts and a manner of communicating them are still present.

After that, you should email it to a few beta readers to collect their feedback and reviews and ask for a foreword before publishing. Writing a book takes time, and there are many factors to consider while creating a product that is worth reading.
Most items have a manufacturing process instead of services requiring competence; they must focus on both scenarios.

We discussed the benefits of preparing before, but in order to develop focus, you must first work on your attention. And it should be an essential component of your day. Create a daily plan that includes your personal life, career, and whatever else you do with your free time.

Let's review key points to help you focus your brain muscle.
Setting specific objectives:

This has already been discussed. Return to the beginning of this chapter if you need to reread it. It would be best to avoid job overload; state what you have on your plate. Because you own your game, presenting your plan with milestones and tasks in execution will get you off the hook.

Create work blocks:

Allocate your Pomodoro spins in blocks of three or four (according to your to-do list), remembering short and long rests. Remember to use your categorization for those chores that have priorities.

Cut down on distractions:

If you are easily sidetracked, you know who you are. You only need a little system to keep you focused; is it your phone, social media, a coworker, or something else? That's a simple repair. You've already considered it. If you can't do everything alone, ask your boss for help and set goals for yourself.

Distractions in the schedule:

I'm not joking, but simply the preceding was... I'm referring to work-related distractions such as your employer or business partner asking you to meet a new client, attending a networking event, or even an essential errand or event that requires your attention.

As a result, when making your to-do list, you must be as precise as possible. You must ensure that all events are considered; this requires adequate preparation.

Many people who want to be more productive have come up with bizarre ideas, such as limiting the number of liquids consumed at work to reduce restroom visits.

The closer you are to the management team, the more quickly you will become sidetracked. Modify yourself to accommodate the distractions.
Turn on your learning mode. In about a week or two, you'll have a pattern to customize your workday and to-do list. When you have discovered several variables, you may readily anticipate when such events will occur.

We sometimes forget that time is a limited resource; we cannot gain more of what it provides daily; we must learn how to use it and distribute it appropriately.

Reducing time wasters will assist you in dealing with frustration; you may incur them in order to preserve resources or money. Such as doing mundane tasks at your wage level; here is a list of time wasters:

Yours.
Your team.
Your employer or business partner.
Your customers or merchants.

Many people say that "time is money," but the reality is that "time is life." You can spend money and get it back, but not time; it's a finite resource that can't be replenished, so let's work SMART.

Build healthy habits

I created a 30-day challenge that will help you change your mindset or attitude toward things in life.

Week 1: Establishing a Strong Foundation

Day 1: Create a to-do list for the day. Make sure it includes both work and self-care tasks.

Day 2: Set a SMART goal for the week. Write it down and make a plan to achieve it.

Day 3: Use a timer to work for 25 minutes without interruption. Take a 5-minute break, then repeat.

Day 4: Prioritize self-care. Get enough sleep, eat a healthy meal, and exercise for at least 30 minutes.
Day 5: Get an accountability partner. Share your SMART goal for the week and check in with each other regularly.

Day 6: Break a large task into smaller steps. Focus on one step at a time.

Day 7: Eliminate distractions. Turn off notifications and close unnecessary tabs or apps when working.

Week 2: Building Momentum

Day 8: Create a to-do list for the day and prioritize tasks by importance.
Day 9: Set a deadline for a project or task. Work towards it throughout the day.

Day 10: Use a timer to work for 50 minutes without interruption. Take a 10-minute break, then repeat.

Day 11: Prioritize self-care. Take a mental health day and do something relaxing.

Day 12: Check in with your accountability partner. Share progress and offer support.

Day 13: Break a task into even smaller steps. Celebrate each small success along the way.

Day 14: Create a distraction-free workspace. Remove anything that might distract you from work.

Week 3: Staying on Track

Day 15: Create a to-do list for the day and set specific deadlines for each task.

Day 16: Set a SMART goal for the month. Write it down and make a plan to achieve it.

Day 17: Use a timer to work for 60 minutes without interruption. Take a 10-minute break, then repeat.

Day 18: Prioritize self-care. Do something you love that energizes you.

Day 19: Check in with your accountability partner. Share progress and offer support.

Day 20: Use a visualization exercise to imagine yourself succeeding at a task or achieving a goal.

Day 21: Find a productivity tool or app that works for you. Test it out and see how it improves your workflow.

Week 4: Finish Strong

Day 22: Create a to-do list for the day and prioritize tasks by urgency.
Day 23: Use a timer to work for 90 minutes without interruption. Take a 15-minute break, then repeat.
Day 24: Prioritize self-care. Take a day off and do something fun.

Day 25: Check in with your accountability partner. Share progress and offer support.

Day 26: Reward yourself for completing a task or achieving a goal.

Day 27: Write down three things you're grateful for. Gratitude can help motivate us to keep going.

Day 28: Review your progress over the past month. Celebrate your successes and identify areas for improvement.

Day 29: Set new goals for the next month. Use what you've learned over the past 30 days to set challenging yet achievable goals.

Day 30: Reflect on the past 30 days. Take note of what worked and what didn't and make a plan for moving forward.

By following this 30-day challenge template, you'll be well on your way to overcoming procrastination and laziness. Remember to stay motivated, celebrate your successes, and be kind to yourself along the way. Good luck!

Okay, I have completed the 30-day challenge. Now what!

I got you covered, my friend. To keep the 30-day challenge going and turn it into a healthy habit that will transform you, here are some actions you can take:

1. **Continue using the SMART goal framework:** Set specific, measurable, achievable, relevant, and time-bound goals for yourself. This will help you stay motivated and focused on your tasks.
2. **Review your progress regularly:** Take some time each week to review your progress over the past week, identify areas where you struggled, and come up with strategies to improve in those areas.
3. **Stay accountable:** Continue to check in with your accountability partner or find a new one if necessary. Sharing your goals and progress with someone can help you stay motivated and on track.
4. **Celebrate your successes:** Take time to celebrate when you achieve a goal or complete a task. This will help reinforce the

positive behaviors you're trying to develop and keep you motivated to continue.

5. **Adapt to your changing needs:** As you progress through the 30-day challenge, you may find that some of the activities or strategies are no longer as effective as they were at the beginning. Be willing to adapt and try new things to keep your momentum going.

6. **Make it a part of your routine:** After 30 days, try to incorporate some of the activities or strategies into your daily routine. For example, if you found that using a timer to work without interruption was effective, try to incorporate this into your daily work routine.

7. **Don't give up:** Remember that developing new habits takes time and effort. Don't beat yourself up if you slip up and miss a day or two. Just pick yourself up and keep going.

By taking these actions, you can turn the 30-day challenge into a healthy habit that can help you overcome procrastination and laziness in the long run and the most important aspect is that you will drop the invisible chain that holds you back from reaching your goals in life.

APPENDIX

Conclusion

Breaking free from false beliefs and mindsets can be a difficult and difficult path, but it can also be one of the most rewarding experiences you can have. Consistent work, commitment, and a willingness to confront and criticize your own views and assumptions are required.

Acknowledging that incorrect attitudes and mindsets can stymie us in many aspects of our lives, including our relationships, employment, and personal development, is critical. These attitudes and ideas may have developed early in our lives as a result of our experiences, upbringing, and cultural and societal influences. But it is critical to recognize that we have the ability to modify them and that little actions taken consistently over time can result in major changes.

The first step in overcoming false beliefs and attitudes is to become aware of them. This necessitates an in-depth assessment of your thoughts, beliefs, and actions. Spend some time thinking about your beliefs about yourself, others, and the world around you. Are any ideas or mindsets preventing you from reaching your full potential? Write them down and consider how they might be affecting your life. This is the whole reason why I have written this book, "The Invisible Chain."

Once you've recognized the incorrect beliefs and mindsets you wish to change, the next stage is to take tiny steps toward a new way of thinking and acting. This could include questioning your assumptions, obtaining fresh knowledge, or simply taking steps toward a new objective.

For example, if you believe you are not good enough, begin by refuting that notion with facts to the contrary. Make a list of all the instances you've succeeded, earned accolades, or accomplished something you're proud of. You can begin to modify your thinking and establish a new, more positive idea by focusing on the information that contradicts your belief.

Another example would be having a scarcity mindset and believing there is never enough for you to succeed. Instead, focus on abundance and seek evidence of all the resources, opportunities, and support available to you. You can begin to perceive new possibilities and opportunities that you may have previously overlooked by adjusting your thinking.

The key to breaking free from false beliefs and mindsets is to take little, consistent steps over time. These activities may appear little at first, but they can lead to big changes in your thinking, behavior, and, ultimately, your life over time.

These are some examples of minor activities you can do to break free from false beliefs and mindsets:

Cultivate gratitude: Set aside time each day to reflect on the things in your life for which you are grateful. This can assist you in shifting your focus from scarcity to abundance and developing a more optimistic outlook.

Seek out new information: Seek out new information and viewpoints to challenge your assumptions. Study books, attend workshops, or engage in discussions with people with opposing views.

Take baby steps toward your new goal: Divide a large goal into small, doable actions, and follow through on those tasks daily. This might help you gain momentum and confidence as you work toward your objective.

Self-compassion: Be nice and sympathetic to yourself, even if you make mistakes or face setbacks. This can aid in developing resilience and reducing the harmful effects of incorrect ideas and mindsets.

Understand that overcoming false beliefs and attitudes is a process, not a destination. It takes consistent effort and dedication, but the rewards are definitely worth it. You may improve your thinking, behavior, and, ultimately, your life by continuously performing modest acts over time. So, take the first step today and set yourself on the path to a brighter future. You've got this!

What should I do next?

The reason why I wanted to write books was with the intention to provide tools and resources for individuals who want to get started and apply the concepts and resources shared. If you are one of those, I'll invite you to join our Private Community and get going with the 30-day challenge. You can find the link on my website https://eliacevedo.com/books/the-invisible-chain/ and get going.

Acknowledgments

I want you to know how much your love and support have helped me finish my book and project. Your constant support gave me the courage to share my knowledge with the world, and I will always be grateful for that.

Your patience and understanding have been worth a lot during those long hours of writing and research. So, thank you to my wonderful wife and kids for giving me strength. Without you, I could not have done all that I have. I hope I can continue to make you happy and proud, just as you've done for me.

About the Author

When it comes to talking about yourself, one of the most difficult and sometimes complex things to express is because you are not your degree or career. And that puts you in a vulnerable position that, in my case, as an Information Technology Professional, we see as a liability because we are used to working behind the scenes and avoiding exposure. I'm a pretty disciplined individual that enjoys sports and working out. I had the opportunity to participate in a variety of sports during my childhood. I've always enjoyed staying fit, whether it was by running early in the morning, going to the gym, riding my mountain bike, or simply working out whenever I could.

My life principles and many concepts that I apply to my life, family, friends, clients, and businesses were taught to me at Saint Francis of Assisi Catholic School, where I was raised. Constantly willing to assist and serve resulted in the success of our company endeavors and people enjoying us, what we do for them, and wanting to be close to us. A blessed life is a gift; my family is the greatest thing I could ever ask for. A charming and hardworking wife, a happy marriage of more than 24 years, and three amazing children make me feel at my best—along with three French bulldogs who keep us all busy.

I enjoy assisting others and witnessing their progress from point A to point B. And transforming their concepts into crystal clear businesses that can provide financial freedom. I advise and teach entrepreneurs how to use technology to gain control and peace of mind. Time management and focus tactics are also discussed for balancing work and family life. In addition, sales and persuasive strategies are covered.

Because it pervades all I do, I'm a living example of discipline, consistency, self-control, and motivation. I enjoy getting up at 5:00 a.m. every day and devoting the first hour of the day to myself and my projects. I've accomplished a lot by devoting only 25 minutes daily to writing two books you can read. Cooking is a third option. I don't have a name yet, but it will be revealed shortly.

We have a unique and important treasure known as time. You will have time to do all you want if you learn to use it to your advantage the best. All examples are spending time with your family, having the finances to travel, and doing what you want without having to wait for a pension when you don't have the energy. I've never considered retiring because I've learned that my path has been a long learning experience. The more I learned, the more I understood how little I knew, which helped me remain humble and accept any new learning opportunity.

If you believe that I can be of assistance to you, please do not hesitate to contact me through my website. Likewise, if you are interested in collaborating with our organization, please let us know, and we will be more than delighted to get in touch with you and determine how we can be of assistance to you or your organization.

Thank you and you got this!

Made in the USA
Columbia, SC
10 July 2023

19995508R00104